OPERATIONS OF THE EIGHTH CORPS

THE RIVER RHINE TO THE BALTIC SEA

A narrative account of the pursuit and final defeat of the German Armed Forces . . . . .

March — May 1945

The Naval & Military Press Ltd

Published by

The Naval & Military Press Ltd
Unit 5 Riverside, Brambleside
Bellbrook Industrial Estate
Uckfield, East Sussex
TN22 1QQ England

Tel: +44 (0)1825 749494

www.naval-military-press.com
www.nmarchive.com

In reprinting in facsimile from the original, any imperfections are inevitably reproduced and the quality may fall short of modern type and cartographic standards.

River RHINE to the BALTIC Sea

This short account of the operations of 8 Corps from the Rhine to the Baltic has been compiled by my Staff from the War Diaries written at the time. It is purely a Narrative of Events, and has been written to place on record the deeds of the formations which, under command of the Corps, took part in this important phase of the operations of the Second British Army leading to the final destruction and surrender of the German forces in North-West Germany.

The calibre of the enemy forces opposing 8 Corps was admittedly not so high as that of those opposed to 12 and 30 Corps on our left (against whom the bulk of the enemy's paratroops were concentrated), and the terrain was more favourable to us, yet these facts cannot detract from the many remarkable achievements of units and formations, and in particular the spectacular performance of 11 th Armoured and 6th Airborne Divisions in reaching the River WESER, a distance of 150 miles, in eight days, which included the crossing of the River Ems and the DORTMUND-EMS CANAL.

Luckily 6th Airborne Division, and 29 Armoured Brigade of 11 Armoured Division had not been implicated in Operation "VERITABLE", which in February had cleared the area between the River MAAS, and the River RHINE, but

6th Airborne Division had taken part in the airborne drop to capture the initial Rhine bridgehead, in which their casualties had been by no means light, and their loss of material was considerable. 29 Armoured Brigade had been out of the line for several weeks, and had been able to carry out much useful training whilst 4th Armoured Brigade had been lent to 11 Armoured Division in their place.

Both formations were in a high state of morale and battle training, and their dash and speed of advance prevented the enemy from organising any coordinated defence on the many major water obstacles that were met. In this they were greatly assisted by the splendid fighting qualities of the 1st Commando Brigade, and the 4th Tank Grenadier Guards from the 6th Guards Tank Brigade, which brigade was operating with the 17th U.S. Airborne Division on our right for the capture of MÜNSTER.

After crossing the River WESER, the Corps was augmented by the inclusion of the remainder of the 6th Guards Tank Brigade, the 15th (Scottish) Division, and the Royals. At this stage it became possible to give the 6th Airborne Division and 4th Tank Grenadier Guards a few days of rather grudgingly accepted rest, during the short halt necessitated by the fact that the Ninth U. S. Army on our right had to regroup so as to complete mopping up in the industrial area of the RUHR.

After the capture of UELZEN, the 5th Division from Italy was placed under command. This formation and the Royals were used to fill the growing gap between the XIII U. S. Corps which was operating Eastwards, and 8 Corps which was operating Northwards and North-Eastwards up to the line of the River ELBE.

Both 15th (Scottish) Division and 1st Commando Brigade had taken part in the initial crossing of the RHINE, and, in view of their experience, were given the task of forcing the crossing of the ELBE. This was by no means an easy operation, as the enemy had extensive observation over the dead flat and coverless marshlands of our side from the escarpment on the East bank of the river. However, enemy resistance and morale had by then been so seriously impaired that the operation was carried out successfully and with very small loss. We were then over the last obstacle, and final victory was assured.

I cannot speak too highly of the work of the Royal Engineers, whose remarkable bridging achievements are set out at the end of the Narrative. Both on the WESER and the ELBE the German Air Force made strenuous efforts to prevent the construction of bridges, but the Sappers, undaunted by casualties, completed their task in record time.

Although these operations, except for the actual crossing of the ELBE, gave little scope for the use of artillery on a grand scale, the support given by R. A. units in small scale actions everywhere was superb, and their mobility and ubiquity was more than ever noticeable.

Finally I must add a word of praise for the Staffs and Services, without whose unflagging efforts the advance from the RHINE to the ELBE would not have been possible. The speed of the advance tested Signal resources to the utmost — the weight fell particularly on wireless (we had no telephone from my Corps H. Q. to Second Army from leaving the Rhine Bridgehead till we arrived at LUNEBURG, a period of 29 days), and also on D.Rs, who went great distances often in areas where mopping up was by no means complete. The strain on the administrative services and administrative staffs was particularly severe — the more so because until the Corps reached CELLE the

Corps main axis was never on better than second-class roads which did not even appear on the ordinary Michelin motoring map. The fact that the Corps was not held up for administrative reasons and that F. M. Cs were always moved forward somehow in time to maintain the flow of ammunition, petrol, supplies, bridge equipment and general stores reflects the greatest credit on the staffs and troops concerned.

It would not be fitting to end this introduction without a special word of thanks to the R. A. F. and particularly to 83 Group. Their exploits and support receive little mention in this account; this is not through lack of appreciation or because we do not realise how much we owe to them, but simply because this is an account of the operations from the Army point of view and because the sources available to us would only in any case allow a most inaccurate and incomplete picture to be given of their ubiquitous activity. It must be enough to acknowledge the debt and to hope one day to be able to read their own account of this period.

Lieutenant-General

Foreword

Introduction

This is the story of the advance of 8 Corps from the bridgehead over the River RHINE to the BALTIC Sea. The advance was remarkable, not only because it was the contribution of 8 Corps to the last battle of the war against Germany and to the final defeat of the German Army on the front of the British Second Army, but also because of the precision and speed with which it was carried out. The momentum of the advance was maintained by day and whenever possible by night for more than a month. It was impossible for the Germans to co-ordinate adequate defence to resist it.

This was the great opportunity for 8 Corps, who, in all the offensives in the Normandy bridgehead, had been frustrated in achieving the longed for breakout. In all the bloody battles around CAEN complete success evaded it, and again at CAUMONT, having achieved a break-out, other Corps of Second Army on the "inside of the bend" and thereby better positioned, took up the pursuit through FRANCE and BELGIUM.

During the winter 1944/45 the Corps carried out useful though unspectacular, operations and closed up to the line of the River Maas. An extended line of some seventy miles was held. Constant patrolling was carried out to harass and bewilder the enemy, but apart from this the Corps was again static. Formations under command during this time were constantly changed over as they were either required for operations elsewhere on 21 Army Group front or for reserve. These formations included 7 U.S. Armoured Division and 75 and 95 U.S. Infantry Divisions.

In writing this narrative a system has been adhered to throughout. The events of each day are given as far as possible as they occurred and the operations of formations and their brigades or battle groups are always described from Right to Left.

At the beginning of the account for each day the intention and tasks of formations for that day are given. Although this system may tend to make the narratives less alive it has been done to make it easier for the reader to understand. Diagrammatic maps showing places referred to in the text have been inserted at the back.

River RHINE to the BALTIC Sea

Operation PLUNDER.

The Rhine Assault and the setting for the break-out to the North German Plains.

In the early months of 1945 operations were successfully carried out by Second Army and Ninth U.S. Army across the River MAAS and the Allied line was closed up to the River RHINE.

21 Army Group was then planning the crossing of the River RHINE, and the codeword given to this operation was PLUNDER, a name that was apt to be taken by some too literally. This operation involved from right to left three Armies, Ninth U.S. Army, Second British Army and First Canadian Army, with the emphasis on Second Army which was to carry out the major assault.

It was clear from the start that 8 Corps was again expected to play only a minor role. The HQ of the Corps was to take over responsibilities for the line of the River RHINE on Second Army front during the preparation period until the Assaulting Corps (12 and 30) were sufficiently established, and until the operation was under way. 8 Corps did a great deal of useful work in getting the stage ready for these assaulting Corps.

A brief description of Operation PLUNDER must be given as it sets the stage for the start of the eventual break-out and advance to the BALTIC.

The object of the operation was to isolate the Northern and Eastern German forces in that great industrial area from the rest of Germany. The task of the three Armies comprising 21 Army Group were as follows: —

Ninth U.S. Army was to assault the River RHINE in the area of RHEINBERG and secure a bridgehead from the junction of the Ruhr and Rhine rivers to BOTTROP and DORSTEN. Thereafter to be prepared to advance to the general line both inclusive HAMM and MUNSTER. This task included the protection of the bridge sites at WESEL and also the RIGHT flank of Second Army.

Second Army was to assault the Rhine in the area XANTEN and REES with two Corps, RIGHT 12 Corps and LEFT 30 Corps, each with one Division up. XVIII U.S. Airborne Corps, consisting of 6 British and 17 U.S. Airborne Divisions, was to drop East of the Rhine as early as possible in the morning after the night assault of 12 Corps. In the employment of these airborne forces it was agreed that the drop was to be within artillery ranges of guns positioned on West bank of River Rhine. It was intended that XVIII U.S. Airborne Corps should link up with the assaulting Division of 12 Corps on the ground on 'D' Day. Meanwhile, 8 Corps was initially to remain responsible for holding the West bank of the Rhine, until both assaulting Corps were ready to control the divisions holding the line. Thereafter its task was to take over from HQ XVIII U.S. Airborne Corps, within seven days, so as to release it for operations in the American Zone. The bridgehead to be established by Second Army was from exclusive DORSTEN to all inclusive BORKEN and AALTEN to DOETINGHEM and HOCH ELTEN feature. Second Army would then be correctly positioned to continue the advance North East towards Rheine and into the North German plains with 8 Corps RIGHT 12 Corps CENTRE and 30 Corps LEFT. 2 Canadian Corps was to be passed through LEFT of Second Army bridgehead and handed back to First Canadian Army when it was in a position to exercise command.

First Canadian Army was to assist in broadening the probable frontage of assault by feints along the Rhine on the left of Second Army, while holding securely the line of this river and the MAAS from EMMERICH Westwards to the sea.

Later, it was to be prepared to advance into Eastern Holland and protect the left of Second Army.

Appreciation of Enemy Strength

Second British Army was opposed by First Parachute Army, consisting of three Corps. 86 Corps was in the South with left 180 Division and right 84 Division in the sector River LIPPE to BISLICH. 2 Para Corps was immediately North of 86 Corps with left 7 Para Division from exclusive BISLICH to inclusive HAFFEN. — Centre 8 Para Division from exclusive HAFFEN to inclusive REES — right 6 Para Division in the sector exclusive REES to inclusive EMMERICH. In reserve 47 Pz Corps was in an area 15 miles North East of EMMERICH with 116 Pz and 15 Pz Gren Divisions under command.

Non-field troops were said to total 58,000 of which 16,000 were supposed to be in defensive positions on the river bank, (but this was not actually the case); 22,000 were, it was thought, to be employed as counter-attack troops, 15,000 defending nodal points and 5,000 immediate reserves.

Development of operations affecting 8 Corps

Tasks given to Corps of Second Army were as follows:—

12 Corps (a) Capture WESEL
           (b) Secure ISSEL crossings
           (c) Capture BOCHOLT
           (d) Capture BORKEN

XVIII Airborne Corps

    (a) Capture and hand to 12 Corps certain key features in area of high ground DIERFORDT and crossings over River ISSEL.

    (b) Gain contact with 12 Corps troops holding WESEL.

    (c) Develop operations Eastwards to the general line DORSTEN — LEMBECK.

    (c) HQ 8 Corps to take over from HQ XVIII U.S. Airborne Corps.

30 Corps

    (a) Capture REES
    (b) Secure crossing over ISSEL. Note: Much further to go than 12 Corps.
    (c) Capture AALTEN.

It had been assumed in the making of this plan that the enemy would resist more strongly close to the vital industrial area of the Ruhr; and that after the river assault 30 Corps would make the most rapid progress, and that a left hook would be bound to develop. 30 Corps was accordingly instructed to use as few troops as possible in the early stages and save everything for the break-out. For the maintenance of a thrust on the left, the road centres of BOCHOLT and BORKEN were essential and 30 Corps were told to be prepared to capture BOCHOLT if 12 Corps were unable to do so. Again it was emphasised that in the event of opposition being too strong 12 Corps was to halt and 30 Corps was to left hook. However, study of the ground and the fact that the German paratroops were holding the line opposite the left of the Second British Army pointed to the possibility that progress might be achieved quicker on the right, which actually was the case.

When the right wing of Second Army had secured the general line DORSTEN to LEMBECK and BORKEN, the boundary between Second Army and Ninth U. S. Army was to be moved North East to the general line from WESEL to BRUNEN thence RAESFELD through HEIDEN and VELEN to COESFELD and on to MUNSTER. At that stage 8 Corps was to hand over it's sector to Ninth U.S. Army and come into reserve.

The prospect of only having a 12 mile advance to carry out was a further disappointment to the Corps and it appeared likely that the history of the Normandy battles would repeat itself by 8 Corps being pinched out. However, this did not damp the optimism of the Corps and merely increased the determination of all to get clear somehow before the pinching out could take place. This was reflected in superhuman (and usually successful) efforts to retain by all possible means equipment, supplies, stores and transport whose removal was constantly threatened and by accepting, at the price of great administrative inconvenience, frequent and uneconomical moves of dumps and installations to conform with the ever closing-in boundaries. This tenacity was later to reap its due reward and prove fully justified since without it the Corps might well have found itself denuded of all that was necessary to take advantage of the break when it came.

Situation when HQ 8 Corps took over on 27/28 March

Second Army was attacking everywhere. Operation PLUNDER had been successful and the enemy were, after severe fighting, thoroughly disorganised by the combined Airborne assault and river crossing.

The situation was a good deal more fluid on the right than on the left. 12 Corps and XVIII U.S. Airborne Corps had joined up on D Day, 24 March, and XVIII U.S. Corps had made considerable progress Eastwards.

The Northern half of DORSTEN had been cleared by 17 U. S. Airborne Division and 6 Guards Tank Brigade. By nightfall on 28th March an armoured regiment group were four miles North East of the town on the main road to HALTERN. By midnight the armoured group had by-passed HALTERN and were still advancing. 3 Para Brigade of 6 Airborne Division had passed through RHADE and reached the outskirts of LEMBECK.

5 Para Brigade were fighting in ERLE.

12 Corps had made good progress against considerably stiffer opposition and their leading armoured cars were on a line 3 miles South West of RAESFELD with tanks to the North of BRUNEN and in the woods South of BOCHOLT. One infantry brigade was North of DINGEN and another brigade attacking on its left.

30 Corps had had a more difficult time but had cleared MILLINGEN and were one mile South of MECHELEN, but was encountering stiff opposition on the autobahn. PRAEST had been occupied by 3 Canadian Division, which was temporarily under command.

After several changes as to the date for the planned relief of HQ XVIII U.S. Airborne Corps, orders were eventually received about midday 27 March for HQ 8 Corps to take over all British troops in XVIII U.S. Airborne Corps.

This included 6 Airborne Division, 1 Commando Brigade and 6 Guards Tank Brigade. It was however decided later that the Tank Brigade less one Battalion should remain with XVIII U.S. Airborne Corps until the capture of MUNSTER. XVIII U.S. Airborne Corps was to remain, and using 17 U.S. Airborne Division and 6 Guards Tank Brigade less 4 Grenadier Guards, was to continue to advance on MUNSTER.

At the time orders were received, Corps HQ had just moved over the Rhine and was in the process of establishing itself in the NE suburbs of Wesel. As the original plan was to take over wireless frequencies from XVIII U.S. Airborne Corps, Corps HQ had no Signal Communication with the formations placed under Command. Furthermore the U.S. Corps HQ was also moving and the Corps Commander was away from his HQ.

This, then, was the set of circumstances and the situation when the Corps took over. It was not yet clear whether the original orders "so far and no further" held good, but it was known that 11 Armoured Division was on its way up from LOUVAIN (BELGIUM) where it had completed its conversion to Comet Tanks (the latest type of cruiser). The Division was to cross the Rhine by the WESEL bridge and concentrate in 8 Corps area. This was a good augury for the future and everyone felt that somehow or other 8 Corps was going to be in to the end. These hopes were confirmed when later next day 11 Armoured Division was placed under command.

Outline of 8 Corps Operations

The breakout from the Rhine bridgehead, the pursuit over 337 miles to the Baltic, and the ultimate defeat of the German Wehrmacht was carried through as one operation. The administrative machine worked faultlessly despite scarcity of transport, the enormous lifts forward of troops, bridging materials and supplies, and the poor quality of the roads allotted to the Corps. Transport was improvised to carry every kind of load and was controlled by Corps.

The line of advance was crossed by a large number of streams and canals and four major rivers. If the advance was to proceed unchecked it was doubly essential to capture bridges intact, for engineering dumps were back behind the Rhine, and ferrying forward would take transport away from the fighting troops.

The Corps was fortunate in the formations it had under command. In particular 6 Airborne and 11 Armoured Divisions, who were outstanding in the way they got themselves forward despite obstacles, lack of roads and limited transport.

Although 6 Airborne Division had undertaken no similar advance before, they were accustomed to making the fullest use of their normal very light scale of transport. 11 Armoured Division had plenty of experience of conducting operations deep into enemy territory with but a semblance of an axis standing behind their advance.

The full narrative account is given in three parts:
    (a) From the RHINE to the WESER
    (b) From the WESER to the ELBE
    (c) From the ELBE to the BALTIC

It is worth noting that apart from a halt of 2 days on the River Leiner, for the Americans to clear up the RUHR, and another on the River ELBE, (where a halt was called to plan a full scale assault), the operations were continuous, apart from minor checks caused by river or canal obstacles An overall speed of advance of over eleven miles per day was achieved from the RHINE to the ELBE, and over sixteen miles per day from the ELBE to the BALTIC.

RHINE to WESER

It was now clear that 8 Corps was not to stop after an advance of 12 miles as originally intended, but was to continue to the River ELBE. Despite the hurried move forward and incomplete and hasty concentration of 11 Armoured Division the Corps was ready and eager for the task so long awaited.

Orders were issued on 28 March for the capture of COES-   29 March
FELD preparatory to a further advance to the River ELBE. 6 Airborne Division on the right with one squadron Inns of Court under command was directed North East on the town itself and 11 Armoured Division on the left was to advance on parallel axis North East to dominate the town from the North, meanwhile maintaining contact with 7 Armoured Division, of 12 Corps, on their left. The advance went well, and 3 Para Brigade of 6 Airborne Division on the Right cleared LEMBECK during the morning 29 March and 6 Airlanding Brigade passed through, reaching the outskirts of COESFELD in the late afternoon. COESFELD was cleared of enemy resistance before midnight, but the road through the town was obstructed by debris from bombing. 11 Armoured Division advanced at first light with 29 Armoured Brigade, after preliminary concentration at ERLE, and by nightfall were at VELEN. The Inns of Court Regiment five miles further ahead operating on the open left flank reached

GESCHER, meeting only scattered pockets of resistance. Contact during the day was established with 7 Armoured Division North East of BORKEN.

1 Commando Brigade, on release by XVIII U.S. Airborne Corps, was held in reserve, moving forward with Corps HQ which was established at ERLE.

Orders were then issued during the day to continue the advance at maximum speed on 30 March to secure within the Corps boundary the general line of the railway from EMSDETTEN to the main road crossing over the railway seven miles South East near GREVEN. Further to seize, intact, if possible, the bridges over River EMS near both those places. 6 Airborne Division was given the axis from COESFELD through LAER and ALTENBERGE to GREVEN 11 Armoured Division on their left were to advance from GESCHER to LEGDEN and SCHOPPINGEN thence through HORSTMAR to the Southern outskirts of BURGSTEINFURT on to EMSDETTEN. HQ 8 Corps was to move on 11 Armoured Divisions axis to OSTERWICK and thence on 6 Airborne Divisions axis.

30 March

6 Airborne Division had a difficult start; owing to rubble in the streets, movement through COESFELD was impossible, and the Division therefore had to make a considerable detour on country lanes to the South of the town rejoining the main road 6 miles East of the town. The Division then turned North and passing through BILLERBEK and ALTENBERGE in the afternoon, reached the river EMS at GREVEN about 2200 hrs. Here both main road bridges had been destroyed, but a small bridge was captured intact.

11 Armoured Division advanced, covered by Inns of Court Regiment, with 29 Armoured Brigade Group in the lead, on both main and subsidiary axis, followed by 159 Brigade Group. On the Right (main) axis good progress was made

through HOLTWICK and as far as HORSTMAR, which was cleared by 1900 hours. The advance was held up by a destroyed bridge between HORSTMAR and BORGHORST. Nevertheless by the evening 4 KSLI of 29 Armoured Brigade Group had made further progress and occupied BURGSTEINFURT. On the Left axis it took most of the morning to clear GESCHER and in the afternoon determined enemy infantry again imposed delay between HOLTWICK and LEGDEN, which lay four miles to the North. Corps HQ moved to KAPELLEN just South East of GESCHER.

In spite of the lack of good, or even direct roads, the speed of advance of the Corps had left the Northern flank exposed over a considerable distance. The responsibility therefore for flank protection was given to 159 Brigade following up.

11 Armoured Division was now re-grouped as follows: —

29 Armoured Brigade Group
  23 H with 8 RB
  3 R Tks with 4 KSLI

159 Brigade Group
  2 FF Yeo with 1 Hereford
  15/19 H with 3 Mons

The rapid advance during the day had overrun fair numbers of enemy and some 1600 Prisoners were taken.

During the night of 30/31 March, 11 Armoured Division built a bridge on the site of the destroyed bridge on the HORSTMAR — BORGHORST road.

Further orders were issued to formations to capture OSNABRUCK preparatory to continuing the advance deep into the Reich. A forecast of routes right up to the River ELBE was sent to formations with as much detail as was known of them at that time. A detailed appreciation of routes is given elsewhere in this history. 6 Airborne Division was given the task of capturing OSNABRUCK, taking the most direct route from GREVEN through LENGERICH and a subsidiary route if required five miles South of the town through NATRUP and OSEDE. 11 Armoured Division still on the left was to advance from EMSDETTEN thence through SAERBECK and DORENTHE to TECKLENBURG and LOTTE over the EMS-WESER Canal at EVERSHEIDE (sweeping just North of OSNABRUCK); thence Eastwards to cut the main road running through OSNABRUCK at a point some ten miles North East of the town and thereby isolate it.

31 March   6 Airborne Division had a difficult task as the high escarpment and thickly wooded feature of the TEUTOBURGERWALD lay across its path and to open the way through, both the town of LENGERICH and the high ground to the North of it, had to be captured.

1 Commando Brigade in Corps reserve was ordered to concentrate forward on 1 April near GREVEN.

Although these orders were issued, tasks for 6 Airborne Division and 11 Armoured Division for 31 March were limited to securing essential firm bridgeheads over the River EMS and the DORTMUND EMS Canal. Added to this, the Northern flank was as open as ever and 11 Armoured Division was therefore rushed back on the left to tie in with forward troops of 12 Corps.

6 Airborne Division advanced and crossed the River EMS and 3 Para Brigade cleared up GREVEN, then, having been relieved by 5 Para Brigade, continued the advance at 1300 hours, reaching the DORTMUND - EMS Canal North West of SCHMEDEHAUSEN by midnight. At 0700 hours 11 Armoured Division entered EMSDETTEN and found the bridge over the River EMS destroyed. Reconnaissance was immediately carried out Northwards to MESUM, where

again the bridge had been destroyed. MESUM, though outside the Corps boundary, presented the best site for bridging, and work was started at midday, protected by a small bridgehead formed by 4 KSLI who had crossed the river unopposed. By late afternoon a Class 40 crossing was completed and 3 R Tks with 4 KSLI followed by 23 H reached the DORTMUND-EMS Canal in the area of RIESENBECK at 1900 hours.

All bridges over the canal had been destroyed by the enemy who were now holding the far bank.

However, 4 KSLI of 29 Armoured Brigade Group managed to cross the canal and before midnight had established a small bridgehead. 159 Brigade Group was providing left flank protection for the Corps, North and West of BURGSTEINFURT with 1 Commando Brigade still further to the West in area of LEGDEN and GESCHER. Inns of Court Regiment was now entirely patrolling on the North flank of 11 Armoured Division, and having captured NEUENKIRCHEN advanced to the outskirts of RHEINE. Another thousand Prisoners were taken during the day, but it was clear that the DORTMUND-EMS Canal was going to impose unwelcome delay on immediate further advance.

Corps HQ moved to LAER.

After three days of rapid progress 1 April saw something of a pause, caused on the right by technical difficulties where 6 Airborne Division was bridging the DORTMUND-EMS Canal, and on the left because 11 Armoured Division, although it had advanced across the canal, was now encountering very much stiffer enemy opposition in the steeply rising country of the TEUTOBURGERWALD.

1 April

6 Airborne Division started to bridge at SCHMEDEHAUSEN at 1130 hours on 1 April, after 3 Para Brigade had cleared the enemy from the area of the site, and com-

pleted a Class 9 bridge by 0530 hours on 2 April. Two battalions of 3 Para Brigade and essential Class 9 traffic were then passed over. Six hours later the crossing had been completed to take Class 40 traffic.

11 Armoured Division on the left was operating outside the left boundary of the Corps and having reached the DORTMUND-EMS Canal at RIESENBECK had started to bridge there.

Despite the fact that this was a 12 Corps axis and would seriously reduce the bridging material available to the Corps for later commitments, it was decided that 11 Armoured Division should continue and complete construction as quickly as possible. The reason for this decision was that 12 Corps was still some way behind on our left, and it was likely therefore that 11 Armoured Division would be clear before 12 Corps could require this route.

4 KSLI (29 Armoured Brigade) was holding the bridgehead at RIESENBECK and a squadron of 3 R Tks was ferried across the canal to join them. This group then advanced North East up the slopes of the TEUTOBURGERWALD, but opposition was severe on the crest of the first ridge and for the time being no further progress could be made.

The Class 40 crossing at RIESENBECK was completed at 1430 hours and 159 Brigade Group crossed immediately, leading with 2 FF Yeo and 1 Herefords who passed through 4 KSLI and 3 R Tks, but stiff opposition was met at once in extemely difficult country. Little progress was made before nightfall and as no reconnaissance had been possible it was decided to wait for daylight before renewing the attack.

Meanwhile, the remainder of 29 Armoured Brigade Group was busy clearing the ground within the Corps boundary between the River EMS and the canal and had captured

SAERBECK, eliminating in the process a battery of eight 88 mm guns.

Corps HQ moved to GREVEN.

Up to this stage in the battle 8 Corps' right flank had been protected by the advance towards MUNSTER of Ninth U.S. Army, who had been in the lead all the time. At the outskirts of MUNSTER a halt was called while negotiations were carried on with the Mayor for the surrender of the town, and also to allow an Airborne Division to be replaced by an Armoured Division. This resulted in 8 Corps taking the lead, with its right flank now also exposed. So, in the evening, 1 Commando Brigade was brought across and made responsible for right flank protection of the Corps from ALTENBERGE to the canal opposite SCHMEDEHAUSEN.

Orders for 2 April were that 6 Airborne Division was to advance and capture OSNABRUCK and 11 Armoured Division to sweep round North of the town and cut the road to the East. Detailed instructions had been given to formations on 30 March. 1 Commando Brigade was still made responsible for the right flank of the Corps from DORTMUND-EMS Canal back to ALTENBERGE. Again the advance on 2 April was relatively slow.

2 April

During the night 1/2 April 6 Airborne Division had secured LADBERGEN and by 0400 hours 2 April had constructed a Class 40 crossing over a stream there.

6 Airborne Division sent 6 Airlanding Brigade by march route through the 3 Para Brigade bridgehead at SCHMEDEHAUSEN directed on LENGERICH which it captured at midday after a sharp fight.. Later it gained the high ground North and North East of the town.

On the left, 11 Armoured Division had a day of hard fighting. Success was gained only by constant manoeuvering of their battle groups in the difficult steep wooded approaches up and onto the TEUTOBURGERWALD. 159 Brigade Group was on the left and attacked at first light, with 3 Mons North onto the high ground and towards IBBENBUREN, and 15/19 H South East to BROCHTERBECK which was cleared during the morning. 3 Mons met further stiff opposition in the woods South West of IBBENBUREN from the cadre of a German NCO School from HANNOVER; this unit had come down on foot to attempt to hold the high ground barring the way to OSNABRUCK. 15/19 H having cleared BROCHTERBECK moved North up the gorge road and then turned NW to try and relieve pressure on 3 Mons. The task of clearing the high ground dominating the road to IBBENBUREN was then left to 159 Brigade Group, whilst 29 Armoured Brigade Group was directed on TECKLENBURG with 23 H and 8 RB leading. TECKLENBURG was cleared by the evening despite opposition from Volksturm armed with Panzerfaust, and 3 R Tks and 4 KSLI passed through the leading group and gained a few more miles to the NE by nightfall.

Things did not go well on the left. 15/19 H were unable to get into a position sufficiently far North West to ease the position of the 3 Mons. Although this ground lay within 12 Corps area and IBBENBUREN was in fact on their axis of advance, it was considered that 3 Mons and 15/19 H should not be withdrawn from the foothold they had gained on the high ground until relieved by troops of 12 Corps. 12 Corps was asked to effect this at the earliest moment as it meant that until this was taken over 11 Armoured Division would virtually be operating as two separate brigade groups.

1 Commando Brigade continued to provide right flank protection for the Corps.

3 April

Formations were given orders for 3 April which were that 6 Airborne Division was to capture OSNABRUCK and 1 Commando Brigade, released from rear right flank protection by the advance of the Americans, was available to 6 Airborne Division to assist in this task. 6 Airborne Division was at the same time to by-pass OSNABRUCK on the South, advance Eastwards and secure the area HOLZHAUSEN and BLASHEIM some 25 miles further on. 11 Armoured Division was to isolate OSNABRUCK from the North East, cut the main road to the East of the town, and to secure the bridges over the EMS-WESER Canal.

On 3 April the earlier speed of advance was once more attained in spite of very bad weather and by the end of the day OSNABRUCK had been outflanked to the South and East by 6 Airborne Division and to the North by 11 Armoured Division, who had reached the EMS — WESER Canal near HERRINGHAUSEN and had secured a bridge intact.

6 Airborne Division's advance was carried out by 3 Para Brigade on the right, swinging South of OSNABRUCK through NATRUP to HAGEN and OSEDE and on the left by 5 Para Brigade who passed through 6 Airlanding Brigade in the area of LENGERICH directed on OSNABRUCK.

Both Brigades moved extremely fast and 3 Para Brigade by midnight 3/4 April had reached WISSINGEN some six miles East of OSNABRUCK destroying a complete AA Bty on the way: 5 Para Brigade reached, and started to clear the Western outskirts of OSNABRUCK in the late afternoon. 6 Airlanding Brigade, was moving up behind 5 Para Brigade, and 1 Commando Brigade in TCVs, was waiting to be called forward to clear the town.

The 6 Airborne Division axis completely broke up just East of the SCHMEDEHAUSEN crossing and serious delay was imposed. 8 Corps HQ was timed to move behind 1 Commando Brigade but in view of the delay it became necessary to pass them so as to get established in the new location. 1 Commando Brigade eventually concentrated just before midnight SW of OSNABRUCK. Corps HQ established itself on the TEUTOBURGERWALD just SW of TECKLENBURG after a slow and chaotic journey due to the road from the Cl 40 bridge at SCHMEDEHAUSEN collapsing.

On the previous night, 2/3 April, 29 Armoured Brigade of 11 Armoured Division on the left of the Corps had at first made remarkable progress, and then was slowed down by bad roads and poor going. However, at 0600 hours, 29 Armoured Brigade's leading troops were approaching LOTTE some five miles due West of OSNABRUCK, and 3 R Tks and 4 KSLI together shortly afterwards captured a bridge intact over the branch of the EMS-WESER Canal at EVERSHEIDE 2 miles North West of OSNABRUCK. At this point a small party of enemy infantry with Panzerfaust cut the road between TECKLENBURG and LOTTE and imposed a delay of an hour before being eliminated by 23 H and 8 RB. Despite this delay 23 H and 8 RB at 1300 hours passed through the bridgehead held by 3 R Tks and 4 KSLI. After disposing of a number of small parties of enemy on their centre line, the leading troop of 23 H with great dash secured the bridge SE of HERRINGHAUSEN intact.

159 Brigade Group on the left was by now some way behind at IBBENBÜREN and 3 Mons had been counter-attacked and driven off the high ground. The battalion suffered a number of casualties and for a time had one company cut off. This company managed to fight it's way clear and rejoned the battalion with 45 Prisoners of War.

It was in this action that Corporal Edward Thomas CHAPMAN won the Victoria Cross. The citation is given here and illustrates the tough in-fighting that was characteristic of the many small scale battles which were fought bitterly to a finish, and which would have seriously hampered the advance if there had not been complete determination to get on quickly.

"On 2 April 45 'D' Company 3 Mon crossed the Dortmund-Ems canal and was ordered to assault the ridge of the TEUTOBURGERWALD, which dominates the surrounding country. This ridge is steep and thickly wooded and is ideal defensive country. It was defended by a Battalion of German officer cadets and their instructors, all of them picked men and fanatical Nazis."

"Corporal CHAPMAN was advancing with his section in single file along a narrow track, when the enemy suddenly opened fire with machine guns at short range inflicting heavy casualties and causing confusion. Corporal CHAPMAN ordered his section to take cover and seizing the Bren gun, he advanced alone firing the gun from his hip, and mowed down the enemy at point blank range, forcing them to retire in disorder."

"At this point his Company was ordered to withdraw, but Corporal CHAPMAN and his section were still left in position as the order could not be passed to them."

"The respite was short-lived. The enemy began to close up to Corporal CHAPMAN and his section and under cover of intense machine gun fire they made determined charges with the bayonet. Corporal CHAP-

MAN again rose with his Bren to meet the assaults, and on each occasion he halted their advance. He had now nearly run out of ammunition, so shouting to his section for more bandoliers he dropped into a fold in the ground, and covered those bringing the ammunition by lying on his back and firing the Bren over his shoulder. A party of Germans made every effort to eliminate him with grenades, but with reloaded magazine, however, he closed with them and once again drove them back causing considerable casualties."

"During the withdrawal of his Company the Commander had been severely wounded and left lying in the open a short distance from Corporal CHAPMAN. Satisfied that his section was secure, he went out alone under withering fire, and carried his Company Commander 50 yards to comparative safety. On the way a sniper hit the Officer again and wounded Corporal CHAPMAN in the hip. When he reached his own lines it was discovered that the Officer had been killed."

"Corporal CHAPMAN refused to be evacuated and remained with his company until the position was restored two hours later."

"Throughout the action Corporal CHAPMAN displayed supreme gallantry and courage. He brought to nothing the attacks of well led determined troops and gave his Battalion time to reorganise on a vital piece of ground overlooking the only bridge over the canal."

"His outstanding bravery assured the capture of this vital ridge."

It was shortly after this that 1 Cheshire were sent forward from 115 Brigade and replaced 3 Mons, which had had a severe mauling.

In the afternoon of 3 April 7 Armoured Division of 12 Corps relieved 159 Brigade Group of the responsibility of the IBBENBUREN area and the brigade concentrated ready to move forward and rejoin the division.

In the late evening of 3 April the Corps received as reinforcements 15 Scottish Division and the remainder of 6 Guards Tank Brigade. The former had been employed under 12 Corps in the original assault crossing of the RHINE and the latter had taken part in the capture of MUNSTER with 17 U.S. Airborne Division under Ninth U.S. Army. Orders were issued to formations for 4 April. The capture of OSNABRUCK was to be completed and thus open up the main Corps axis: and the advance to the East was to be continued to secure further crossings over the EMS-WESER Canal at one and the same time. 6 Airborne Division, therefore, in addition to clearing OSNABRUCK (using 1 Commando Brigade) was, in contact with 11 Armoured Division East of the town, to open up the main route and then secure the area of HOLZHAUSEN and BLASHEIM near LUBBECKE and crossings over the EMS-WESER Canal North and North East of LUBBECKE. At the same time 11 Armoured Division was to protect the left flank of the Corps, uncovered again as a result of our rapid advance. 11 Armoured Division was ordered to push on from its small bridgehead at HERRINGHAUSEN some sixteen miles, as far as RAHDEN.

6 Airborne Division advanced rapidly Eastwards and cleared WEHRENDORF and LUBBECKE. 3 Para Brigade was in the lead, and by 1500 hours was only 4000 yards short of the River WESER, but found that MINDEN was

4 April

quite strongly held. An attempt to get through the town to the river was unsuccessful. It therefore took up positions in the Western outskirts of the town and made contact with U.S. troops, on the right, who had made a very rapid advance.

6 Airlanding Brigade following up 3 Para Brigade during the day had a small battle with two companies of enemy infantry and some anti-tank guns, and having disposed of them concentrated North West of LUBBECKE after dark. 5 Para Brigade remained holding the Western outskirts of OSNABRUCK whilst 1 Commando Brigade assaulted the town in the early hours of the morning. After two hours fighting opposition died down, and by midnight all of the town up to the line of the canal, which runs through it from South to North, had been occupied. That same evening 1 Commando Brigade in OSNABRUCK reverted to Corps control thus relieving 6 Airborne Division of responsibility on the OSNABRUCK area and releasing 5 Para Brigade to rejoin the Division.

11 Armoured Division on the left advanced out of the bridgehead at HERRINGHAUSEN on the 4th of April and soon encountered opposition on the high ground less than a mile ahead. 29 Armoured Brigade Group was in the lead and soon dealt with this opposition, and other parties of enemy along their route to RAHDEN, where stiffer resistance was met and cleared by late afternoon.

The brigade resumed the advance on two routes. 3 R. Tks and 4 KSLI on the right advanced and cleared DIEPENAU, and 23 H and 8 RB advanced and took up positions just before dark some 3 miles to the North of that town. 159 Brigade Group moved forward from OSTERKAPPELN on the EMS — WESER canal and was made responsible for the exposed divisional centre line. 2 FF Yeo and 1 Herefords were used for this task and were based centrally on LEVERN. The Inns of Court Regiment was again patrolling energetically to the North and was relieved of the Westward part of this task by the arrival of the forward armoured cars of 11 Hussars of 7 Armoured Division, as far East as a point some eight miles North East of OSNABRUCK. 15 (S) Division, who had concentrated during the morning at GREVEN, was ordered to move forward again to LENGERICH using 11 Armoured Divisional axis. 227 Brigade started to move forward but was completely blocked by the whole of 7 Armoured Division operating under 12 Corps to whom permission had only been given, to move a small maintenance column of vehicles on this route.

At this time the only crossing the Corps had over the DORTMUND — EMS canal was at DORENTHE on 11 Armoured Divisions axis, as the road East of SCHMEDEHAUSEN on 6 Airborne Division axis had broken down so badly, that it was fit only for light, unladen, returning traffic.

It was of very great importance to maintain the momentum of the advance, and not only were 15 (S) Division required forward, but also bridging materials and supplies which were now stationary on the road. This misunderstanding was thus especially aggravating at this particular moment in that it delayed the forward concentration of a vital formation, seriously slowed down the turn round of maintenance lorries at a time when maintenance runs were already very long and delayed the arrival in the forward areas of stores which were urgently required.

Great numbers of enemy were overrun during the 4th of April and 2,500 Prisoners were taken. Many thousands more were wandering aimlessly Westwards, bewildered by the speed of the British advance.

Corps HQ moved forward to BISSENDORF.

5 April   Orders were again issued to formations for the 5th of April. 6 Airborne Division was to advance and secure a bridgehead over the River WESER at PETERSHAGEN, and protect the right of the Corps, while 11 Armoured Division was to advance and secure a bridgehead over the river in the area of STOLZENAU, large enough to start bridge construction. Neither formation was to move main bodies forward of any bridgehead they succeeded in establishing over the R. WESER. 15 (S) Division was ordered to complete its concentration in the area GREVEN and LENGERICH, to clear the wooded area North of the road DORENTHE to LENGERICH, and be prepared to concentrate just West of the WESER on the 6th of April. 1 Commando Brigade was ordered to finish the task of clearing OSNABRUCK and be prepared to send one Commando Battalion forward to 6 Airborne Division to take over and hold LUBBECKE.

It was clear that, when captured, so large a town and vital communication centre as OSNABRUCK could not be left without a garrison. It was equally clear that 1 Commando Brigade was likely to be badly needed forward in the near future and that to leave one Commando Battalion behind as a garrison for the town would be most unsatisfactory. 77 Medium Regiment which had been left behind after crossing the Rhine so as to lighten the force was therefore ordered to move forward urgently to relieve the Commando Brigade, which on relief was ordered to join 11 Armoured Division.

6 Airborne Division using 3 Para Brigade, again attacked MINDEN in the early morning of the 5th of April and after some fighting the town was cleared at midday. But that afternoon, as it was within the American boundary, it was handed over to troops of Ninth U.S. Army. While 3 Para

Brigade was fighting for MINDEN, 6 Airlanding Brigade advanced from LUBBECKE, and reached the WESER at PETERSHAGEN at 1400 hours, and eliminated opposition there. In the afternoon the river was crossed opposite WIETERSHEIM upstream from PETERSHAGEN.

By midnight WIETERSHEIM had been cleared and one battalion and one company were over the WESER.

5 Para Brigade, released from OSNABRUCK, moved forward and concentrated at FRIEDEWALDE, five miles SW of PETERSHAGEN.

At 0700 hours 5 April, 11 Armoured Division advanced on the WESER, two brigades up, with 159 Brigade Group on the Right and 29 Armoured Brigade Group on the left. 159 Brigade Group reached the WESER at SCHLUSSELBERG at 1115 hours and 1 Herefords, crossing the river against slight opposition, were established with one company on the far bank at 1415 hours.

29 Armoured Brigade Group with 23 H and 8 RB leading reached the WESER at STOLZENAU some three quarters of an hour before 159 Brigade. Some opposition was also encountered here, but at 1315 hours 8 RB crossed the WESER under cover of smoke and had two companies established by 1530 hrs.

No sooner had bridging begun than attacks developed on the two companies of 8 RB which held the bridgehead opposite STOLZENAU. Bridging was seriously impeded by attacks from the air and harassing fire from the ground.

The attack on the bridgehead was beaten off but the two companies of 8 RB were not well placed to meet another strong attack.

The Corps had advanced so swiftly that forward airfields were left far behind and air cover could be provided only at short and infrequent intervals. This was inadequate for protecting the bridging sites which were obvious targets for the enemy air force.

15 (S) Division, using 227 Brigade, completed their task of clearing the large wooded area astride the 6 Airborne Division axis (which was also the Corps axis) while 1 Commando Brigade completed the clearance of OSNABRUCK by the late afternoon. 46 RM Commando was then sent to clear the road running out to the East where it made junction with, and was placed under command of, 11 Armoured Division.

Corps HQ moved to HILLE.

A further 3,500 Prisoners were accounted for in the day and in addition a large scale trek of unescorted and unchecked self disarmed Wehrmacht moving Westwards was in progress.

This then was the situation at the conclusion of the first part of the offensive. The River WESER had been reached on a twenty mile front and two small bridgeheads had been achieved.

The Corps, measured by the most direct route, had covered 150 miles in eight days. In this advance, formations of the Corps had not only overcome all enemy resistance but had overcome successively these obstacles: River EMS, DORTMUND — EMS Canal, the steep and thickly wooded escarpment of the TEUTOBURGERWALD and the EMS — WESER Canal. Many thousands of prisoners had been taken. The vital communications centre of OSNABRUCK had been captured — by far the largest German town so far occupied by Second Army — and so had very many inhabited places varying from small villages to medium sized towns such as MINDEN.

No mention has so far been made in this narrative of the Military Government problems which were beginning to arise; to give any long description of these would, in a purely military narrative such as this, be out of place; yet these problems, which increased continually as the advance moved further East, must be kept in mind as part of the background of the Corps' operations; they were in fact an integral part of these operations and even from time to time had a very direct effect on them. The staff and detachments available, specifically for this work, were quite insufficient in numbers to cope fully with all their tasks in spite of extremely hard work and heroic efforts; inevitably much was also done by units and formations on their own, usually with much initiative and commonsense.

Briefly the military government problems at this stage fell into two categories. The first and easier one was the problem of maintaining some kind of government and order among the German population overrun so that military operations should be impeded as little as possible; this sort of work usually including the appointment of Burgomasters, telling the police to continue with their work, preventing looting and generally ensuring that food distribution continued and that essential public services were kept going. Generally speaking apart from the labour of getting round and giving instructions this aspect went easily enough as the population and officials were docile and only too keen to carry out orders. The second problem, and by far the more difficult, was the mass of displaced persons and ex-prisoners of war which were being uncovered during the advance. Every effort was made to persuade the DPs to stay in their camps till orderly arrangements for them could be made but, quite understandably after a long period of confinement and restriction this advice was not taken in most cases and the roads were crowded with refugees — those with homes in the West marching purposefully in that direction while Eastbound DPs roamed about aimlessly. Collecting centres were established as it was essential to keep the roads clear and also to ensure law and order by prevention of marauding and pillage. Inevitably a considerable quantity of military transport and supplies were diverted to the maintenance and organisation of these displaced persons at a time when the speed of the advance made such a demand very difficult. The strain on the administrative services was thus considerably increased but it was a claim which in the name of humanity could not but be met cheerfully by all.

These problems will not be mentioned again in this narrative — they were a constant factor in operations and now progressively increasing in importance and number; they should therefore be considered as a background and it must be remembered that though doubtless much was not done which should have been it reflects great credit on all concerned that in the general hurry and turmoil so much was nevertheless achieved. What could have become a serious threat to operations was dealt with efficiently enough to turn it into merely a source of hard work and a certain amount of inconvenience.

River WESER to River ELBE

6 April

Orders for 6 April were given to formations to enlarge their bridgeheads over the River WESER at PETERSHAGEN and STOLZENAU. 6 Airborne Division was to construct two crossings at PETERSHAGEN, one Class 40 and one Class 9, and 11 Armoured Division one Class 40 at STOLZENAU. Enemy resistance had hardened on the River WESER and in particular at STOLZENAU in the North.

Throughout the advance the right of the Corps had always been freer and therefore was always ahead of the left. The enemy had tried to hang his right flanks on the sea, and stretch his forces South so as to contain our advance. 11 Armoured Division was up against the Southern extremity of his defensive lines, again and again; and had it not been for the speed of the advance, the enemy would have had time to harden and extend this line, and thereby have checked, at least for a while, the brilliant advance of the 6 Airborne Division.

During the night 5/6 April, 6 Airborne Division continued to ferry 6 Airlanding Brigade over the WESER at PETERSHAGEN and by midday on 6 April its bridgehead had been extended as far East as the railway line from LAHDE to FRILLE. 5 Para Brigade was in position to protect the construction of the two bridges at PETERSHAGEN. In the afternoon two small counter attacks were put in by the enemy infantry, supported by 3 to 4 tanks in each case, and the Class 9 bridge which was just South of the Class 40 was hurriedly completed so as to send at least one or two anti-tank guns across. Typhoons were called up and attacked these enemy groups and no further activity was seen in this area.

During the same night 11 Armoured Division continued to bridge at STOLZENAU under machine gun and artillery fire. 11 Armoured Division clearly required more infantry to deal with the continuous enemy pressure on the Northern flank and to free the lorried infantry brigade to advance with the armour. Accordingly, 45 RM Commando — the leading unit of 1 Commando Brigade now released from OSNABRUCK and hurrying forward — was placed under command of 11 Armoured Division on its arrival late on the night 5/6 April. This unit was put across the river early in the morning to strengthen up and relieve troops of 159 Brigade on the South East of the STOLZENAU bridgehead where opposition was stiffest.

When the STOLZENAU bridgehead looked secure, 159 Brigade Group withdrew their two companies of 1 Hereford who had been forming a small bridgehead at the ferry site to the South. Bridge construction at STOLZENAU was being continually interrupted by shelling and persistent air attack. Two bombing attacks by JU 88s in the afternoon caused the sappers some 40 casualties and destroyed a large amount of pontoon equipment and badly cratered the bridge approaches. Insufficient undamaged material remained at the site to complete the bridge and work had to be temporarily suspended. On the open Northern flank the Inns of Court Regiment was in contact with enemy South of BARENBURG in the morning, but was able to hand over this area to troops of 12 Corps at midday.

By the same evening (6 April) 45 RM Commando was in somewhat precarious contact with the two companies of 8 RB.

The enemys position was centred on the village of LEESE, and two successive attacks failed to dislodge him. The first, made by 45 (RM) Commando, succeeded in gaining only 200 yds. The second was intended as an operation for the whole Commando Brigade subsequent to their crossing the river to relieve 8 RB during the night 6/7 April, but the relief itself, and the evacuation of the two companies was only accomplished with considerable difficulty, and the attack was soon pinned down.

A 'most immediate' signal was received from the Army Commander which was as follows — "Keeping your right flank on the WESER—ELBE canal you will advance to the River LEINE at once and secure bridgeheads in the area WUNSTORF and NEUSTADT. No advance of main bodies will take place beyond River LEINE for the present".

Orders were therefore issued for 7 April for 6 Airborne Division, Right and 11 Armoured Division, Left, to continue the advance to the river LEINE. 6 Airborne Division to secure WUNSTORF, the airfield at that place, NEUSTADT, and, if possible, seize a bridge intact over the River LEINE, or failing that, a bridgehead large enough to allow construction of a Class 40 crossing. 11 Armoured Division was to seize a bridge intact over the River LEINE at MANDELS-LOH or NIEDERSTOCKEN, or failing that make a bridgehead of sufficient depth to allow a Class 40 crossing to be built at one of those places.

7 April

6 Airborne Division was ordered to advance on 7 April, although it was evident that 11 Armoured Division could make little progress, until the stiff enemy opposition had been overcome around the WESER bridgehead. During the

previous night 6 Airborne Division had extended its bridgehead Eastwards over the railway line and in the morning Northwards to WINDHEIM and DOHREN. The Class 40 crossing was completed by the early hours of the morning, and 5 Para Brigade passed through 6 Airlanding Brigade, directed on the crossings over the River LEINE at BORDENAU and NEUSTADT. 15 (S) Division Reconnaissance Regiment under command of 6 Airborne Division was operating ahead of 5 Para Brigade in anticipation of 15 (S) Division taking over on the right from 6 Airborne Division. Extremely rapid progress was made against patchy enemy opposition and in the late afternoon 15 (S) Division Reconnaissance Regiment succeeded in seizing the BORDENAU bridge intact, while 5 Para Brigade aproached WUNSTORF. 15 (S) Reconnaissance Regiment East of the river then swung North to NEUSTADT and by 1800 hours 5 Para Brigade had closed up to BORDENAU and reached NEUSTADT from the West, capturing the bridge intact. The NEUSTADT bridge was subsequently destroyed by a delayed action charge which went off while troops of 7 Para Battalion were crossing. Few casualties were incurred.

11 Armoured Division's bridgehead over the River WESER remained about the same except that 1 Commando Brigade was now up. To allow freedom of manoeuvre for an attack on LEESE, 11 Armoured Division was given the use of the Class 40 bridge at PETERSHAGEN and 159 Brigade Group moved South, crossed the WESER, and turned Northwards. Contact was made with the enemy almost at once in LOCCUM but it took all day to clear the enemy from this place. By late evening, 159 Brigade Group had passed through DOHREN and HEIMSEN and reached the outskirts of LEESE. No further progress was possible despite support from 29 Armoured Brigade Group on the WEST bank.

Enemy reserves had appeared on 11 Armoured Division's sector which included 2 Marine Division, 352 Division and an SS replacement battalion. West of the WESER the North flank was still very open and 75 Anti-Tank Regiment was sent North in the morning to seize and hold the road centre of LEMKE, and prevent the enemy operating against our Lines of Communication. This Regiment had reorganised its two forward batteries as infantry and these, after overcoming some stubbornly defended posts, established themselves at LEMKE.

11 Armoured Division ordered 1 Commando Brigade to attack and capture LEESE during the night 7/8 April. This was achieved by 2300 hrs. A further attempt was made to continue bridge construction but persistent and accurate shelling of the site made this an impossible task.

During the 6 and 7 April, 15 (S) Division with 6 Guards Tank Brigade, less 4 Grenadier Guards, under command, moved forward from the GREVEN and LENGERICH area. They completed their forward concentration just West of PETERSHAGEN by midnight on 7 April. Transport for this move had to be scraped together from other formations, as it was required again at the earliest moment for further tasks. All the time the distance between the Corps and the forward army engineer and supply dumps was increasing and the turn-round of transport was considerable.

On 8 April, 6 Airborne Division, still keeping 4 Grenadier Guards, was ordered to consolidate its bridgehead over the River LEINE and to operate with light forces Northwards, if possible seizing intact the bridge at HESTORF to assist the future advance of 11 Armoured Division.

8 April

11 Armoured Division had orders to clear up the enemy and to bridge either at STOLZENAU and SCHLUSSELBERG, and to continue the advance.

15 (S) Division was to remain in reserve in the area West of PETERSHAGEN.

6 Airborne Division strengthened its hold on the River LEINE and mopped up parties of enemy between the WESER and the LEINE. The Class 40 crossing was started at NEUSTADT.

During the morning a squadron of 15 (S) Division Reconnaissance Regiment operating under 6 Airborne Division moved upstream and captured the bridge intact at RICKLINGEN. A Panther tank was known to be West of the LEINE in this area so the squadron's only anti-tank gun was sited facing WEST. At about 1400 hours the enemy attacked the bridge from the East with one Tiger, two Panther tanks, and infantry mounted on them. The Reconnaissance Squadron beat off this attack and the enemy retired, leaving twenty dead on the battlefield. Our own troops suffered casualties in men and equipment. That evening the bridge was handed over intact to troops of XIII U.S. Corps.

On the morning of the 8th April, 29 Armoured Brigade Group crossed the WESER at PETERSHAGEN and moved North making contact with 1 Commando Brigade in LEESE.

Enemy resistance was determined but ill-organised. 29 Armoured Brigade Group made good progress and advanced Northwards through REHBURG and HUSUM reaching LINSBURG at last light, still in contact with the enemy. 159 Brigade Group followed close on the heels of 29 Armoured Brigade and passing through REHBURG swung away to the North East; SCHWEEREN, EILVESE and HAGEN were cleared during the afternoon and about last light the Brigade reached the river LEINE at HELSTORF and NIEDERNSTOCKEN; the bridges at both these places were found to have been destroyed.

Corps HQ moved to WOLPINGHAUSEN.

The ill-fated bridge site at STOLZENAU was abandoned and Royal Engineers of 15 (S) Division, placed under command of 11 Armoured Division, started to construct a Class 40 crossing at SCHLUSSELBURG ferry site a few miles further upstream.

Orders were given to 6 Airborne Division on 9 April to continue to hold their bridgehead over the River LEINE at BORDENAU and NEUSTADT and to operate energetically with light forces East of the river.

9 April

During the day it succeeded in extending the existing bridgehead to include BRINK and SCHARREL to the East of NEUSTADT. The bridge at NEUSTADT was completed.

11 Armoured Division was ordered to secure a bridehead over the River LEINE and in this it had some difficulty. It was involved in further fighting West of the LEINE and was also opposed from the East bank. To avoid an assault crossing, 159 Brigade sent 15/19 H and 1 Cheshire across the bridge at BORDENAU and this group turned North making no contact with the enemy until it reached a suitable bridge site at ESPERKE, some four miles North of HELSTORF. The enemy at ESPERKE were eliminated and the advance continued to BOTHMER, where the bridge was found to be destroyed. Bridging was started at once at HELSTORF.

29 Armoured Brigade Group advanced from LINSBURG North Eastwards, and having advanced eight miles, met determined opposition from SS troops in STEIMBKE. NIENBURG, further to the West on the WESER, was surrendered by the Mayor to a small force sent by 11 Armoured Division. Inns of Court patrols pushed on to ERICHSHAGEN.

Other patrols of Inns of Court had reached as far North as HOLTORF, five miles North of NIENBURG, and LICHTENHORST, five miles North of STEIMBKE. Troops of 12 Corps took over responsibility for the area of LEMKE and 75 Anti-Tank Regiment moved to rejoin the division. Royal Engineers of 15 (S) Division completed the Class 40 crossing at SCHLUSSELBERG.

10 April   Orders for 10 April were that 6 Airborne and 11 Armoured Divisions were to improve their bridgeheads over the River LEINE. 15 (S) Division was ordered to concentrate forward between the River WESER and the River LEINE preparatory to taking over the running on the right from 6 Airborne Division when the Corps advanced. Limited advances only were made, therefore, and 15 (S) Division Reconnaissance Regiment, still operating under 6 Airborne Division, made contact with U.S. forces to the South at BISSENDORF and MELLENDORF both places being then taken over by 3 Para Brigade, and also FUHRBERG, which was found clear.

On 11 Armoured Division's sector there was still a fair degree of enemy opposition to all forward movement. 159 Brigade Group advanced North, clearing SCHWARMSTEDT after a stiff fight. 29 Armoured Brigade Group gave left flank protection to the advance of 159 Brigade Group.

During the afternoon 1 Commando Brigade under 11 Armoured Division concentrated in the area of SCHWARMSTEDT and BOTHMER, preparatory to assaulting over the River ALLER and securing the road bridge at ESSEL which was still intact.

That night 1 Commando Brigade crossed the river below ESSEL making use of the railway bridge which had been only partially destroyed, and succeeded in establishing a small bridgehead from which to launch further attacks

South East to take the road bridge from the rear. At 0200 hours the enemy blew the bridge, but fighting against determined opposition, 1 Commando Brigade secured the site of the bridge and a perimeter of 1200 yards.

During 10th April a directive was received from the Army Commander. An extract from this directive is given below: —

Extract from Directive from Army Commander to Corps Commander

1. It is probable that the advance in strength to the River ELBE will start on 14 April. I cannot tell you yet what your RIGHT boundary on the River ELBE will be, but on your way to the river you will include CELLE and UELZEN.
2. In the meantime: —
   (a) Keep your right flank in touch with the left of the leading troops of Ninth U.S. Army. How far forward they will go before 14 April I don't know, but I am told they will take HANNOVER to-day.
   (b) Keep your front from solidifying by making at least a small advance each day; and
   (c) help the advance of 12 Corps to RETHEM in every way you can.
3. I am transferring the Royals to you. Chief of Staff will send you the expected time of arrival.

On the evening of 10 April a second directive was received from the Army Commander which stated: —

1. Ninth Army is continuing its advance East without a pause. Its main weight will be on the axis from HANNOVER to BRUNSWICK and MAGDEBURG. The left hand Corps which will get under way rather later than

the main drive, will have its left directed on SALZWEDEL and WITTENBERG.

2. The present intention of 12 U.S. Army Group is to construct their main bridgehead in the MAGDEBURG area, and (if required to do so) they will advance on BERLIN from MAGDEBURG. They do not propose to bridge the River ELBE North of STENDAL.

3. Second Army will continue to advance to the River ELBE at once with its right directed on DOMITZ and cavalry (8 Corps and U.S.) filling the gap between DOMITZ and WITTENBERGE. Whether a bridge will be built by us at DOMITZ has not yet been decided.

4. When the River ELBE has been reached by Second and Ninth Armies the right of Second Army will move North West to include the river crossing at NEU-DARCHAU. Ninth Army will take over the river line from WITTENBERG to exclusive DARCHAU.

5. 8 Corps will: —
    (a) Secure CELLE and the line of the River ALLER within Corps boundary at once; and
    (b) it will then secure UELZEN without reference to the advance of 12 Corps on its left, but keeping contact with the left of Ninth Army.

6. 12 Corps will: —
    (a) secure bridgeheads over the River ALLER within the Corps boundary.
    (b) place one division North of the river WESER on the line OTTERSBURG to ACHIM to mask BREMEN.
    (c) secure the line SOLTAU to ROTENBERG, keeping touch with left of 8 Corps on the line SOLTAU to UELZEN.

52 (L) Division, 4 Armoured Brigade and 3 Division will be passed to the East of WESER and ALLER as soon as possible.

Left flank protection BRAMSCHE via BASSUM to DREYE until 30 Corps advance.

Orders for 11 April were issued to formations which were that 15 (S) Division was to pass through 6 Airborne Division and

11 April

(a) advance and secure CELLE, then UELZEN, and
(b) construct a Class 40 crossing at CELLE over the River ALLER.

11 Armoured Division was
(a) to secure BERGEN
(b) protect the left flank of the Corps and secure EBSTORF, and
(c) construct a Class 40 crossing at either ESSEL or WINSEN over the River ALLER.

6 Airborne Division was to move up behind 15(S) Division and clear the wooded area astride the axis of their advance.

15 (S) Division advanced with 46 Brigade on the right and 227 Brigade on the left. 15 (S) Division Reconnaissance Regiment, who had reverted to command, covering the division's advance.

This Regiment found itself out of contact with the enemy at first light and advanced through GR BURGWEDEL and ENGENSEN before regaining contact at the level crossing at EHLERSHAUSEN South of CELLE.

46 Brigade was held up all day and into the night by enemy holding EHLERSHAUSEN and 227 Brigade, after overcoming stiff opposition on the road between FUHRBERG and CELLE, was held up on the FUHSE canal some three miles South of CELLE.

47

11 Armoured Division with 159 Brigade Group operating on the right, cleared woods to the West of the road which runs from BERKHOF Northwards to ESSEL, and also succeeded in getting part of the Cheshires across the River ALLER four miles to the East of ESSEL.

Heavy enemy counter attacks supported by artillery and armoured cars were put in all day against the small bridgehead held by 1 Commando Brigade.

During the evening 4 KSLI crossed the river to reinforce the brigade while a short distance upstream 1 Cheshire also crossed and established a separate bridgehead.

During the night 11/12 April Royal Engineers constructed rafts to enable tanks to be ferried across the river.

Corps HQ moved to NEGENBORN.

12 April   Orders were issued that for 12 April. 15 (S) Division was to secure CELLE and construct a Class 40 crossing there over the River ALLER. 11 Armoured Division was to secure its bridgehead over the River ALLER at ESSEL. A considerable area of wooded and uncleared ground now lay between 15 (S) Division, whose left axis ran along the road East-North-East from FUHRBERG to CELLE, and 11 Armoured Division, whose right axis was that of 159 Brigade Group on the road from BERKHOF to ESSEL. No lateral roads through had been cleared. The Situation was further aggravated by the fact that parallel axes running North East over the River ALLER did not exist, and the intended bridge sites at CELLE and ESSEL were eighteen miles apart. WINSEN, it is true, was only seven miles from CELLE but, once having become committed to a bridgehead at ESSEL, it was considered undesirable to abandon it; to have done so would have exposed the left rear of 11 Armoured Division and, in any case, bridging equipment was at this time

so short that it is doubtful whether the demands resulting from starting another bridge could have been met.

Only a short advance was achieved on the 12th April, but the important thing was that 15 (S) Division succeeded in capturing CELLE and completing a Class 40 crossing there over the River ALLER.

On 11 Armoured Division sector two emissaries under a flag of truce came over the bridge at WINSEN in the morning. Their object was to negotiate the orderly handing-over of the Concentration Camp at BELSEN. These emissiaries stated that the German Army had taken over responsibility for the camp two days before; they were most emphatic that they had never been allowed in the camp before and had been horrified to see the conditions. They emphasised that they had not the means at their disposal materially to improve conditions and that it was highly desirable in the interests of humanity that we should take it over as soon as possible and that there should be no risk of the place becoming a battlefield or a target for artillery fire. Apart from the humanitarian side they emphasised that typhus was rife in the camp and that it was in the interests not only of the German Army and civilian population but also in that of the British Army that the inmates should not escape and wander loose all over the country.

The Germans, therefore, proposed that the area of the camp should be inviolate and respected by both sides. They would undertake to define this area on maps and mark and picket the limits on the ground, and in addition would give us an unopposed bridgehead at WINSEN and the bridge intact.

These proposals were satisfactory up to a point but suffered from two major objections. First, the main road ran through the proposed area and no other road was available. Secondly, it would have been possible for the Germans to sit just on the far edge of the area in such a way that our operations would have been grossly hampered by restricted freedom of movement and possibly inability to deploy artillery within range.

That afternoon therefore the B.G.S. went across to the enemy lines to take counter-proposals. Whilst these negotiations were in progress it was agreed that there would be no fighting or shooting into or out of an area within 4,000 yds of WINSEN, the bridge at which the B.G.S. was to rendez-vous and thence be conducted to the German HQ.

Fighting, however, at ESSEL, continued as fiercely as ever. The rafts for ferrying the tanks were completed by 0900 hours and one Squadron of 3 R. Tanks crossed to support 1 Commando Brigade. During the day 45 and 46 (RM) Commando attacked towards HADEMSTORF and met with determined resistance and could not get into the village but meanwhile 1 Cheshire moving westwards from their small bridgehead succeeded in linking up with the brigade.

The B.G.S. was taken to a German HQ. which he believed to be 1 Para Army, somewhere near SOLTAU, and interviewed the Chief of Staff, Oberst von Mantei.

(Note: Some days later it was discovered that the HQ visited was that of Army Group Blumentritt.)

The counterproposal put forward by 8 Corps was briefly
(a) The camp area should be inviolate by both sides and picketted as suggested by the Germans.
(b) The Germans to be allowed to withdraw and the British to advance through the Camp area but neither side to stop or operate within it except for the essential purposes of guarding and administering the camp.

(c) The Germans to withdraw about 10,000 yds NORTH of the defined inviolate area so that we might redeploy on the far side.

Oberst von Mantei was not empowered to agree to this and therefore telephoned the Headquarters of the Reich Fuhrer S.S.

These proposals were turned down by the Germans because, as they truthfully pointed out, agreement would force them to withdraw also from RETHEM on 12 Corps front since this position would have been completely turned.

Further negotiations on these lines would clearly have continued to be abortive and finally a modified agreement was reachet at about 2100 hours. The terms of agreement were as follows: —

(a) the Wehrmacht undertook to do all it could to improve conditions in the camp and to continue to administer it until such time as the tide of battle forced them to withdraw from their present positions.

(b) when forced to abandon their present positions all German troops were to withdraw NORTH of the camp as rapidly as possible. Both sides might use the roads through and in the immediate vicinity of the camp.

(c) Neither side would now or during withdrawal and advance, shoot into or out of the camp area. (The Germans while refusing to agree to withdraw to a set distance beyond the camp, gave a verbal undertaking that they would not redeploy NORTH of it in such a way as to force us to deploy artillery or other weapons in the Camp area; it was understood that if they did so the agreement could and would be broken by us.)

(d) The Germans would define the camp area on the ground with notice boards in German and English and leave disarmed picquets with white flags and armbands on the main roads in. Moreover they would leave a guard of 600 Hungarian and about 100 German troops on the camp itself. We undertook to treat the German troops honourably and return them to the German lines within one week of taking them over.

(e) The Germans agreed to retain, by force if necessary, the SS Administrative Staff; this was necessary since they alone had any idea of the internal workings of the camp and could be made to produce records, statistics and so on. It was made quite clear that no kind of undertaking was entered into with regard to our subsequent treatment of these SS. (The Wehrmacht were only too happy to accede to this demand and clearly quite enjoyed the prospect of carrying it out — an interesting side-light on the relations of Wehrmacht and SS)

Such information as was available with regard to conditions in the camp and the administrative situation, was then handed over to allow us to make the necessary plans to cope with the situation. Information was very sketchy and vague but nevertheless made it quite clear that conditions were truly appalling and would need the most energetic action by us as soon as we arrived.

The full story of BELSEN has been recorded and it is not the intention here to repeat descriptions of the nauseating bestiality which was uncovered there; it is enough to say that the written word is inadequate to record conditions as they were found.

Nevertheless this record would not be complete without a word of tribute to those troops of the Corps who, within the limited resources available to an army engaged on active operations at the end of a very long L of C, did so much during the first few days after the capture of the camp on the 15th of April. A considerable part of the administrative effort of the Corps was diverted at a time when it could very ill be spared. 63 A/Tk Regiment RA were placed in charge of the camp and laboured heroically, assisted particularly by the Medical Services and RASC, to produce some kind of order in the camp and some immediate improvement in conditions. It must be admitted that resources available allowed little more than the alleviation of the worst suffering and the first efforts to stem the tide of death in the camp. Yet considerable success in these two aims were achieved before, about a week later, responsibility for the camp was taken over by HQ Second Army.

On 13 April 15 (S) Division was ordered to advance from its bridge over the River ALLER at CELLE and secure UELZEN. 11 Armoured Division was to continue to bridge the River ALLER at ESSEL.

13 April

During 13 April and the night 13/14 April 15 (S) Division made extremely good progress and reached the outskirts of UELZEN at 0645 hours on the morning of 14 April. The main road was found to be blocked by unexploded bombs and a diversion WEST of the road was used through HOSSERINGEN and SUDERBURG. 227 Brigade was leading the advance with 46 Brigade clearing on either flank.

During the night 12/13 April the situation at ESSEL eased somewhat and bridge construction went ahead rapidly and was completed by 0500 hours 13 April.

29 Armoured Brigade's leading group consisting of 3 R. Tanks and 4 KSLI crossed the river and attacked Northwards but were held up shortly afterwards by enemy in the woods immediately north of the river.

159 Brigade attacking eastwards met with greater success and by last light were approaching WINSEN. 15/19 H and 1 Cheshire overcame strong opposition and destroyed during the day eleven anti-tank guns and captured more than two hundred prisoners. 1 Commando Brigade continued to hold the enemy at ESSEL, and in fact remained there until the advance of 12 Corps on the left reduced the enemy pressure and enabled them to be withdrawn.

14 April The intention of the Corps for 14 April was

- (a) to advance and establish itself on the River ELBE in the area opposite LAUENBURG
- (b) capture LUNEBURG and operate North and West to assist the advance of the remainder of the Second Army.

On the morning of 14 April 227 (H) Infantry Brigade encountered enemy opposition and by 1000 hours was fighting in the Southern outskirts of UELZEN and in the woods two miles due SOUTH of the town. Pressure was kept up during the day and shortly after midnight the Brigade, with 6 RSF under command, put in an attack on the town. Strong opposition was encountered from enemy infantry supported by tanks and no progress could be made. UELZEN, in fact, resisted all attacks for four days, and it was not until 18 April that the enemy were finally forced to abandon it.

46 Brigade was still clearing the flanks of the divisional axis and 44 Brigade was moved forward to open up the axis leading North from WEYHAUSEN. Here again, the main axis ran through large forests and lateral communications between 15 (S) Division and 11 Armoured Division had to be opened up. 11 Armoured Division was experiencing difficulty and 159 Brigade with 1 Cheshire in the lead was still

two miles East of WINSEN. 1 Herefords were then directed to carry out an outflanking movement and reached the WINSEN -- OSTENHOLZ road by 2200 hours and fought their way into WINSEN.

During the night 14/15 April 2 Glasgow Highlanders and a Squadron of 15 (S) Reconnaissance Regiment were heavily counter attacked in STADENSEN and NETTLEKAMP just SOUTH of UELZEN and suffered some loss. The attack was launched by a battle group of Panzer Division Clausewitz. They had orders to break through our line southwards and join up with their forces encircled in the Harz Mountains. An ambitious programme for a battle group without reinforcement, administrative set-up, or hope of secure axis. Nevertheless, this group struck South and reached NIENWOHLDE, where a violent battle ensued with 2 Glas H, who drove the enemy back with considerable losses, which amounted to 12 SP guns, 20 75-mm guns, 11 half tracks and 2 armoured cars. Losses on our side amounted to 2 17-pdr guns, 22 carriers, 10 half tracks and 31 miscellaneous vehicles.

Corps HQ moved to HABIGHORST.

The orders issued for 15 April were that 15 (S) Division was to complete the capture af UELZEN and prepare to advance East to HITZACKER and NEUDARCHAU on the River ELBE.

15 April

6 Airborne Division was to concentrate South East of UELZEN, relieve troops of 15 (S) Division there, and be prepared to advance the following day directed on LUCHOW and DANNENBERG. They were given the additional task of clearing the wooded area between 15 (S) Division and 11 Armoured Division, thus opening lateral communication.

11 Armoured Division was to continue its advance from WINSEN, via BERGEN, (which took them close to BELSEN) to HERMANNSBURG, LINTZEL, and WRIEDEL and secure EBSTORF.

During 15 April 46 (H) Infantry Brigade was relieved on the right and left flanks by 6 Airborne and 11 Armoured Divisions respectively, and moved up to relieve 227 (H) Infantry Brigade which was holding a line immediately SOUTH of UELZEN. Opposition on 11 Armoured Division's sector began to crumble. This may have been largely due to the the agreement in regard to BELSEN.

159 Brigade Group advanced North East from WINSEN and cleared in succession HOLTHAUSEN, HASSEL, SULTZE, and HERMANNSBURG, and by last light leading elements had reached a point just North of MUDEN, where the bridge was found destroyed.

29 Armoured Brigade Group advanced northwards from WINSEN and found BERGEN clrar. The Brigade then split into two battle groups, one advancing East to capture DOHNSEN and BONSTORF, while the other continued to advance northwards and reached MARBORSTEL.

BELSEN camp was entered and agreements and arrangements made by the Germans had been adhered to.

16 April   Orders for 16 April were that 15 (S) Division was to complete the capture of UELZEN, while 6 Airborne Division was to capture LEHMKE and HAMSTEDT, and cut off the enemy's retreat from UELZEN by cutting the roads leading East from UELZEN and making contact with 11 Armoured Division. 11 Armoured Division was to continue its advance to secure EBSTORF to the North West of UELZEN and again advance to the general line LUNEBURG to

AMELINGHAUSEN, thus protecting the left of the Corps. LUNEBURG was to be secured if enemy resistance was not too great, but if strongly held was to be isolated. FORST MUNSTER was to be skirted and no attempt made to clear it of enemy.

The direct attack on UELZEN had temporarily failed and 15 (S) Division was positioning it's troops for an attack on 17 April. 44 (L) Brigade with a Squadron of 4 Grenadier Guards was ordered to cross the river STEDERAU in the area of NIENDORF and STEDENDORF and work round the Eastern flank of the town. This manoeuvre was successful and pockets of enemy resistance encountered were overcome and by early morning 17 April the leading troops of 44 (L) Infantry Brigade were established on the line of the road UELZEN to GROSSLIEDERN.

6 Airborne Division having relieved 46 Brigade of 15 (S) Division, occupied the villages of KAHLSDORF, LEHMKE and ESTERHOLZ, thus further isolating the town from the South East.

During the night 15/16 April 159 Brigade Group had gained a bridgehead at MUDEN and started to build a Class 40 crossing. The bridge was completed at 1030 hours on 16 April and 159 Brigade Group (right of 11 Armoured Division) advanced, clearing SCHMARBECK and WICHTENBECK, and reached EIMKE by last light. 29 Armoured Brigade, which was on the left of 11 Armoured Division, had gone Northwards from MARBOSTEL, and turning Eastwards had got a bridgehead with 8 RB over the stream at REDDINGEN. All the bridges were destroyed in this area and the ground was intersected with streams; it was decided, therefore, to bring 29 Armoured Brigade back and across the bridge at MUDEN. 29 Armoured Brigade carried this out quickly and by last light had reached and secured its objective, a remarkable feat.

Corps HQ moved to HOSSERINGEN.

The recent rapid advance had again exposed both flanks of the Corps, and so the Royals, who were now under command were given the task of operating on the Southern flank and maintaining contact with U.S. troops. The Inns of Court operated both on the left flank back to the leading troops of 12 Corps, and also in the gap between 15 (S) Division and 11 Armoured Division.

17 April On 17 April the Army Commander informed the Corps Commander that the Russians had started their drive to the West and it was therefore essential to reach the ELBE as early as possible, and there stop the vast numbers of refugees moving Westwards in front of the Russian advance. The Russian advance North of BERLIN was likely to be swift as the greater number of German Divisions were in defensive positions to the South. Orders had already been issued for 17 April and 15 (S) Division was to mount an attack and capture UELZEN at midday, if practicable, or failing that, at first light on 18 April.

6 Airborne Division was to continue with the task of cutting all the roads East from UELZEN and was to make contact with 11 Armoured Division (the Western arm of the pincers) at EMMERDORF, five miles North of UELZEN on the railway line. 11 Armoured Division was to establish itself more firmly at EBSTORF and WEIDEL, make contact with 6 Airborne at EMMENDORF and cut the road North of LUNEBURG. 15 (S) Division closed in on UELZEN during the day, 44 Brigade occupying LIEDERN. 6 Airborne Division outflanked the town to the North East, and, passing 3 Para Brigade through 6 Airlanding Brigade, seized RATZ-

LINGEN, RIESTEDT and MOLZEN. 11 Armoured Division advanced and 23 H and 8 RB cleared BARUM against strong opposition most efficiently and got into a position to dominate the main road and railway to LUNEBURG. 1 Commando Brigade, still under 11 Armoured Division, was positioned at WRIEDEL to protect the left flank.

On 17 April at 1900 hours 15 (S) Division using 46 (H) Infantry Brigade started it's attack on UELZEN. 46 (H) Infantry Brigade made some progress into the Southern outskirts of the town that night.

On 18 April 15 (S) Division finally captured UELZEN, 44 Brigade clearing the part of the town East of the river, and 46 Brigade the Western half. Enemy opposition had eased considerably, but houses were booby trapped and snipers were not completely cleared until that evening.

18 April

6 Airborne Division improved its position to the East of UELZEN and made contact at EMMENDORF with troops of 29 Armoured Brigade, who were then relieved by 1 Commando Brigade to allow the division to advance Northwards again with right 29 Armoured Brigade and left 159 Brigade. By midday 29 Armoured Brigade, moving very rapidly, had cleared BIENENBUTTEL, MELBECK, passed through WENDISCH EVERN and cleared the Eastern part of LUNEBURG against light opposition. By nightfall patrols had reached NEETZE, ten miles to the East, and SCHARNEBECK, six miles to the North East of the town. 159 Brigade Group advancing from WRIEDEL, entered LUNEBURG from the West in the middle of the afternoon, and captured both bridges intact. One company of the Cheshires was left in the town as garrison and the Brigade advanced to BARDOWICK, four miles, and to ROTTORF, seven miles North West of the town.

19 April   The intention now was to close to the River ELBE immediately. 15 (S) Division was ordered to advance as early as possible on 19 April and get established on a narrow front on the ELBE in the area LAUENBURG and BLECKEDE. 11 Armoured Division was ordered to advance and secure the line of River ELBE from opposite LAUENBURG to inclusive WINSEN, handing over later the sector LAUENBURG to TESPE to 15 (S) Division.

6 Airborne Division was to remain concentrated East of UELZEN carrying out reconnaissance on the roads UELZEN — LUCHOW and UELZEN — DANNENBERG; to assist in this 5 Divisional Reconnaissance Regiment was placed temporarily under its command.

5 Division, who had been concentrating South of UELZEN for the past three days, was to be prepared to pass through 6 Airborne Division on 20 April on the axis UELZEN, ZERNTEN, NEUDARCHAU, establish itself on the River ELBE between inclusive NEUDARCHAU and exclusive BLECKEDE and later take over the latter town from 15 (S) Division.

It took three days (19 to 22 April) to close up to the River ELBE. On 19 April 15 (S) Division moved 227 Brigade forward; relieved troops of 11 Armoured Division in the area North East of LUNEBURG and occupied the villages of LUDERSBURG, ECHEM and HITTBERGEN. 29 Armoured Brigade cleared the enemy from the approaches to the bridge over the River ELBE at LAUENBURG, but the bridge was blown up when our troops were within 200 yards of it. 15 (S) Division troops relieved 29 Armoured Brigade here and the brigade withdrew and concentrated West of LUNEBURG. 159 Brigade Group advanced on the left and cleared WINSEN by that evening.

20 April On the 20 April, 5 Division, now on the right of the Corps, advanced with 17 Brigade on the right and 13 Brigade on the left against varying opposition. 15 (S) Division was now in the centre and 227 Brigade succeeded in capturing ARTLENBURG and AVENDORF against stiff opposition, and also occupied HOHNSTORF and TESPE. 46 Brigade moved up on the right of 227 Brigade. 159 Brigade, of 11 Armoured Division, on the left of the Corps, cleared the road from WINSEN to NIEDERMARSCHACH where contact was made with a party of enemy, who were eliminated.

During the day the Wehrmacht guard from BELSEN camp was ferried across the River ELBE at NIEDERMARSCHACH and returned to the German lines in accordance with the agreement made.

Corps HQ moved to the South West suburbs of LUNEBURG.

21 April On 21 April 5 Division made good progress and 13 Brigade on the left had captured BARSKAMP, and was astride the railway just South of BLECKEDE. 17 Brigade on the right was still some way back experiencing difficulty in the area of the FORST GOHRDE. 15 (S) Division cleared the loop of the river between BLECKEDE and LAUENBURG.

22 April By the evening of 22 April the Corps was everywhere established along the line of the River ELBE, except at NEUDARCHAU itself, which, after a final brisk fight, was cleared on 23 April.

For the ten days from 13 to 22 April Prisoners were taken at the rate of more than 1,500 each day.

The River ELBE had been reached on a 38 mile front, and an attempt to seize a bridge intact had very nearly succeeded. The river was almost as great an obstacle as the

RHINE and so there was nothing for it but to prepare a detailed plan to assault and secure a bridgehead large enough to cover ferry and bridge construction.

An advance of 103 miles had been made in fourteen days and some 19,000 prisoners of war had been taken. Two major water obstacles had been overcome and many great areas of forest had been traversed. The left bank of the River ELBE was ours, and LUNEBURG, UELZEN, CELLE and many hundreds of smaller towns and villages lay behind, cleared of the enemy.

River ELBE to the BALTIC Sea

The assault crossing of the River ELBE had been considered as early as 14 April when the Corps was still South af UELZEN. Now detailed orders were sent out and the operation was named "ENTERPRISE".

Not a great deal was known of the strength of the enemy, but it appeared that he had prepared no defensive line on the ELBE and that the troops he had available totalled some twenty ersatz battalions, possibly backed up by 245 Division. In the area it was estimated he had approximately 100 Heavy A.A. and 160 Light A.A. guns in all.

The river, however, was 900 feet wide and presented a formidable obstacle. The NORTH bank opposite ARTLENBURG was a steep and wooded escarpment while on the SOUTH of the river the country was dead flat marshland totally devoid of cover. The enemy thus had every advantage as far as observation and concealment were concerned and our approaches and proposed bridge sites were in fact completely dominated from his positions. It was appreciated, however, that the plateau North of the ELBE would provide good road communication and good going for tanks once a secure footing had been made.

The Army Commander defined the object of the operation as "the capture of a bridgehead over the River ELBE to allow 12 Corps and XVIII U.S. Corps to pass through". Circumstances, however, changed this plan, as 12 Corps was not far enough advanced and XVIII U.S. Corps operated over its own bridges further to the East.

The Corps plan was to secure a bridgehead over the River ELBE to include Point 62 (West of BOIZENBURG), ZWEEDORF, POTRAU, MUSSEN, SCHWARZENBECK, BRUNSTORF, DASSENDORF and the bend in the River opposite STORE.

The plan was divided into a number of phases, but these phases would not necessarily follow each other, but would be developed as opportunity offered, the aim all the time being to get on.

These were the phases of Operation ENTERPRISE.

Phase I. 15 (S) Division with 1 Commando Brigade under command to assault and secure a bridgehead at LAUENBURG and ARTLENBURG to cover bridge and ferry construction. To secure intact, if possible, bridges over the ELBE-TRAVE canal to the East of LAUENBURG.

Phase II. 15 (S) Division to extend bridgehead to include KRUZEN.

Phase III. 15 (S) Division to extend the bridgehead further still to include DALDORF, LUTAU and Point 86 (East of GEESTHACHT).

Phase IV. 15 (S) Division to pause and regroup, handing over the Eastern sector of the bridgehead to 6 Airborne Division, who would then extend the bridgehead further Eastwards to include Point 62 NOSTORF and ZWEEDORF.

Phase V. 6 Airborne Division on right to secure the final limit of the bridgehead, using 15 Brigade of 5 Division to secure that part of their bridgehead

West of ELBE TRAVE Canal.

To seize two bridges some eight miles North of LAUENBURG over the canal.

15 (S) Division to secure final limit of the bridgehead on the left of 6 Airborne Division, and, using a Brigade of 12 Corps, clear GEESTHACHT and the high ground round HOHENHORN.

D-Day for the operation was 1 May but was put forward to 29 April in order to forestall the hordes of refugees believed to be converging on LUBECK in front of the Russians. H-Hour was fixed for 0200 hrs. The river assault was to have been supported by an air drop but the change of date gave insufficient time for arranging this. However, it was not considered essential to the success of the operation.

Every moment was needed to bring forward bridging assault equipment and ammunition for the operation. Army dumps were many hundreds of miles back, but the railway between CELLE and LUNEBURG had been got into operation, and thereby the turn-round of the transport was shortened. It was a race against time to get everything set for the assault. Medium and Fighter Bomber plan had to be timed in with the river assault. Approaches to the river for LVTs had to be made and sign boarded. Traffic Control for LVT ferry DUKW's and bridge sites had to be co-ordinated to ensure smooth and rapid build-up for the next operation which was the break-out from the bridgehead.

The break-out was planned to be carried out by 5 Division on the right directed via MOLLN on LUBECK and 11 Armoured Division on the left directed via TRITTAU on BAD OLDESLOE, so as to dominate all roads leading out of LUBECK to the North and North West. 6 Airborne Division, after crossing the ELBE - TRAVE Canal, was to come under orders of XVIII U.S. Airborne Division, which was operating on the right of 8 Corps whilst 15 (S) Division protected the left flank of the Corps.

29 April   At 0200 hours on 29 April, Operation ENTERPRISE began; and 15 (S) Division with 1 Commando Brigade under command assaulted across the R. ELBE. The weather was stormy, and the medium bomber effort had to be cancelled owing to cloud. The artillery bombardment before the assault, was adjusted, and was increased where necessary, to cover any targets not now having been accounted for by the bombers. Opposition was only moderate and 1 Commando Brigade with 7 Seaforths under command, assaulting on the right from about half way between LAUENBURG and ARTLENBURG, crossed the river, and moving round North of LAUENBURG captured the bridge over the ELBE-TRAVE Canal intact by 0700 hours, and by 0835 had cleared LAUENBURG itself. During the afternoon BUCHORST was cleared, and the second bridge a little further North over the ELBE-TRAVE Canal was captured. This bridge had been damaged by the enemy but it was still possible to use it.

On the left of the 15 (S) Division ELBE assault, 44 Brigade had crossed either side of the ARTLENBURG ferry site and by 0800 hours had cleared SCHNAKENBEK and by evening had occupied the villages of JULIUSBURG, KRUKOW and GULCOW. 46 and 227 Brigades followed up the assault, and the former thrust Northwards from LAUENBERG, while the latter turned Westwards. 46 Brigade cleared KRUZEN before midday and in the afternoon captured BASEDOW and the two hill features North of KRUZEN, and were in contact with the enemy holding DALLDORF; the leading elements of 227 Brigade were North West of GRUNHOF by the end of the day.

Construction of the two bridges, one of Class 9 at LAUENBURG and the other of Class 40 at ARTLENBURG, was started at the earliest moment that morning, and despite delay caused by persistent enemy fighter-bomber attacks, the Class 9 was finished and opened for traffic by the evening, a first class achievement by the Sappers.

Casualties in the assault had been light, although enemy artillery was active. The weather improved during the morning and the RAF were able to give excellent close support, engaging a number of targets which included enemy strong points in JULIUSBURG, and also railway guns, which were shelling the bridging sites, and were out of range of our artillery. During the day 1400 prisoners were taken.

On the right of the Corps, 5 Division was relieved on the line of the ELBE by 82 U.S. Airborne Division, under command of Ninth U.S. Army, and were thus free to concentrate in an area immediately South of the Class 9 (right hand) bridge. During this time both 5 Division and 11 Armoured Division were preparing to cross into the bridgehead, and get set for the break-out to LUBECK and the BALTIC. This break-out operation was known as VOLCANO and was a continuation of ENTERPRISE. There was to be no pause whatsoever, and all preparations to pass the break-out formations through the ELBE bridgehead were made before ENTERPRISE had started.

On 30 April, 15 (S) Division was told to extend its bridgehead and secure SCHWARZENBEK cross-roads before dawn of the First of May. It was through this place, SCHWARZENBEK, that 11 Armoured Division was to strike North to the sea. 6 Airborne Division was to relieve 15 (S) Division of the right hand sector of the ELBE bridgehead and extend this eastwards over the ELBE—TRAVE Canal.

30 April

5 Division Right, and 11 Armoured Division Left, were to be prepared to move over the Class 9 and Class 40 bridges on the morning of 1 May.

During 30 April, 15 (S) Division succeeded in extending its bridgehead, and 44 Brigade, moving Northwards, cleared LUTAU and accepted the surrender of enemy troops holding WANGELAU two miles further North. 46 Brigade was then passed through on this axis and secured SCHWARZENBEK by that evening.

227 Brigade, meanwhile, made only slight progress Westwards towards GEESTHACHT but captured HAMWARDE to the NE and also cleared KOLLOW. Just after midday 6 Airborne Division was given the use of the Class 9 bridge. 3 Para Brigade was sent over first, followed by 15 Brigade (belonging to 5 Division but temporarily under command of 6 Airborne Division). 3 Para Brigade was directed Eastwards, and made excellent progress to just beyond BOIZENBURG, where its advance was checked until first light to avoid confusion with U.S. troops crossing the ELBE in that area. 15 Brigade moved Northwards and relieved 46 Brigade and 1 Commando Brigade of 15 (S) Division in the area of DALLDORF immediately West of the ELBE –– TRAVE Canal.

By midday the Class 40 crossing at ARTLENBURG had been completed, in spite of comparatively heavy casualties to the Sappers working on it from air attacks. 4 Grenadier Guards under command 15 (S) Division were sent across first but experienced difficulty in negotiating the steep, winding exit on the far bank.

It was the Corps Commander's original intention to pass 11 Armoured Division through as soon as the road centre of SCHWARZENBEK had been cleared by 15 (S) Division. However, progress had been so good that he decided to speed it up.

Just before midnight 30 April / 1 May, therefore, 11 Armoured Division started to cross with one group of 29 Armoured Brigade (23 H and 8 RB) leading, followed by a group of 159 Brigade, 3 R Tks and 1 Herefords. Both these groups advanced Northwards but as the bridge over the stream just North of CULZOW was destroyed, both groups had to use a very minor road running North East to SCHWARZENBEK, towards which they advanced through the night.

On the first of May Operation VOLCANO, the break-out, was to begin, — some 36 hours earlier than had been anticipated. 5 Division on the Right was to resume command of 15 Brigade, debouch through 6 Airborne Division and advance North East through MOLLN and RATZEBURG to LUBECK.

1 May

11 Armoured Division on the left was to debouch through 15 (S) Division, secure REINFELD and BAD OLDESLOE, swing North East to isolate LUBECK from the North, and then operate against LUBECK to assist in its capture by 5 Division.

15 (S) Division was to protect the left of the Corps, and to clear the Eastern part of the SACHSENWALD forest to facilitate the advance of 11 Armoured Division.

6 Airborne Division was to be prepared to extend the bridgehead over the ELBE—TRAVE Canal and to come under command of XVIII U.S. Airborne Corps.

The break-out started on the first of May. On the Corps extreme right, 6 Airborne Division continued to advance rapidly eastwards, and early in the morning linked up with American troops, who had assaulted across the ELBE, East of BOIZENBURG. 6 Airborne Division, together with the Scots Greys, of 4 Armoured Brigade, and 6 Field Regiment passed to command of XVIII U.S. Airborne Corps of Ninth

U.S. Army. 5 Division completed concentration and resumed command of 15 Brigade. Its break out was, however, now delayed until 2 May, so as to give time for 6 Airborne Division to get clear to the East of ELBE--TRAVE Canal.

11 Armoured Division debouched through 15 (S) Division and advanced two brigades up; on the Right 29 Armoured Brigade, and on the Left 159 Brigade. 29 Armoured Brigade overcoming, with the help of 15 (S) Division, opposition in SCHWARZENBEK, was at first held up by stubborn enemy resistance at a destroyed bridge at SAHMS, which was not finally cleared until that night. However, a way round was found, and part of the leading group (23 H and 8 RB) of 29 Armoured Brigade continued the advance, clearing a number of villages against moderate resistance, and reached BORSTORF. This represented an advance of approximately 10 miles, and the second group (2 FF Yeo and 1 Cheshire) of 29 Armoured Brigade was passed through. By this time opposition was negligible, and 2 FF Yeo Group reached WENTORF, a further advance of some six miles; thence a squadron group was sent to SANDESNEBEN, which was cleared; the group withdrew to WENTORF for the night.

159 Brigade Group on the left was having a more difficult time, and was held up to start with 2000 yards North West of SCHWARZENBEK by defended road blocks and mines. During the morning an advance of six miles to BASTHORST was nevertheless achieved and an advance of a further four miles was made in the afternoon to TRITTAU. A number of villages were cleared and at dusk the leading group consisting of 3 R Tks and 4 KSLI was fighting in GRONWOHLD.

On the extreme left, 15 (S) Division was unable to extend the bridgehead further West, but the enemy, concerned about large dumps of gas shells and chemical warfare stores in the area of GEESTHACHT, offered to surrender the town. This was accepted by 15 (S) Division and the occupation of the village took place shortly afterwards. This was highly satisfactory as one of 8 Corps tasks was to capture GEESTHACHT so as to allow 12 Corps to bridge there without having to undertake an assault crossing. The town was handed over to 158 Brigade (53 (W) Division) which, having crossed the Class 40 bridge and been placed under command of 15 (S) Division to seize the place, was actually in the process of planning to carry out the attack.

Corps HQ moved to WANGELAU.

Orders were given for 2 May. 5 Division was to advance on LUBECK as ordered, using the Royals to reconnoitre well out to the East over the ELBE—TRAVE Canal and so keep in touch with XVIII U.S. Airborne Corps. 11 Armoured Division was to push on as fast as possible, and 15 (S) Division was to continue to clear the SACHSENWALD, and hand 158 Brigade with GEESTHACHT back to 12 Corps.

2 May

On 2 May, 5 Division having completed their concentration during the night advanced Northwards. 13 Brigade with 2 Wilts in the lead passed through 15 Brigade which had cleared POTTRAU after a stiff fight. 13 Brigade entered MOLLN at 1100 hours, where scattered resistance was overcome, and two hours later had a company in RATZEBURG and was just short of EINHAUS, three miles further NorthWest. 2 Wilts made further progress during the afternoon and by midnight had reached GR GRONAU about 5 miles South of LUBECK. The two other battalions of 13 Brigade were positioned at RATZEBURG and MOLLN, and 17 Brigade Group following up had passed two Battalions through MOLLN by nightfall. The Royals maintained contact with 6 Airborne Division on their right, which was now operating under the Americans.

During the night 1/2 May, heavy rain and traffic caused the roads behind 11 Armoured Division to collapse and great difficulty was experienced in getting supplies forward. This delayed the start next morning. Eventually however the advance was resumed with 29 Armoured Brigade on the Right, and 159 Brigade on the Left. By mid-morning, 29 Armoured Brigade (2 FF Yeo and 1 Cheshire) had reached SIEBENBAUMEN, an advance of about 6 miles from WENTORF.

Meanwhile 159 Brigade, advancing from GRONWOHLD, which they had been unable to clear the previous evening, reached BARKHORST on the HAMBURG—LUBECK autobahn.

The Corps Commander was at this time told by the Army Commander that the capture of LUBECK might result in the Germans throwing in their hands. The surrender of HAMBURG was already being negotiated.

Orders were now given to 11 Armoured Division to seize LUBECK with all speed. 29 Armoured Brigade was given this task while 159 Brigade was directed on BAD OLDESLOE and REINFELD. 29 Armoured Brigade advanced at midday and 2 FF Yeo Group advanced along the autobahn into LUBECK, which was reached at 1550 hours. There was some sniping in the town, but no other resistance was met and the bridges were secured intact.

159 Brigade meanwhile, after encountering light opposition South of the autobahn, secured BAD OLDESLOE and REINFELD.

15 (S) Division during the day continued to clear the SACHSENWALD area. Early in the morning German emissaries contacted the Division with proposals for a large scale surrender. During the afternoon GOC 15 (S) Division brought the Chief of Staff of Army Group BLUMENTRITT

to Corps HQ to put forward the enemy proposals. The German proposal was that the British should undertake not to close the routes across the ELBE—TRAVE Canal to the mass of civilian refugees streaming West to escape the Russian advance; in return the Germans were willing to surrender all troops operating against 21 Army Group between the Danish frontier and the river EMS (the envoys intimated that German forces in Holland and Denmark would probably follow suit but that their HQ was not in a position to give orders to these forces). To deal with proposals on this scale was obviously far beyond the competence of a Corps HQ involving as they did the whole of 21 Army Group front. The proposals were accordingly passed to the Army Commander and arrangements were made for a meeting between him and representatives of the germans to take place at LAUENBURG next day. (NOTE: — This proposed meeting in fact never took place since, in the interval, negotiations on a much higher level which concerned the surrender of the whole remaining Wehrmacht had already begun). The German envoys were then sent back to their own lines; nothing concrete had been achieved but it was clear to those who knew of these approaches that the campaign in North West Europe was rapidly approaching its end.

For the three days, 29 April to 1 May, Prisoners of war taken averaged about 1,500 a day, but on 2 May German surrenders were wholesale. In LUBECK alone 11 Armoured Division had counted 15,784 by 2200 hours and their total for the day was estimated at 18,000, including 5 Generals, while 5 Division estimated their total to be 16,000, including the German 245 Division which surrendered complete.

There is little more then to this story. The Baltic was reached at TRAVEMUNDE at 1100 hours on 3 May by 11

Armoured Division and the following day a message was received from Army saying that hostilities would cease on all Second Army fronts at 0800 hours on 5 May. We had looked for Victory for so long that it was hard to understand that 'here it was' and the war against Germany was at an end.

Order of Battle during the advance from the RHINE to the BALTIC

Formations and major units which operated under the Corps during the period are given below: — (NOTE: space forbids the inclusion in this list of the very many administrative units, without whose invaluable work the advance could never have succeeded)

1. **11 ARMOURED DIVISION**

    HQ RA 11 Armoured Division
    13 RHA
    151 Fd Regt RA
    65 A Tk Regt RA
    58 LAA Regt RA

    HQ RE 11 Armoured Division
    612 Fd Sqn RE
    13 Fd Sqn RE
    147 Fd Pk Sqn RE
    10 Br Pl RE

    HQ 29 Armoured Brigade
    Inns of Court
    3 R Tks
    23 H
    15/19 H
    2 FF Yeo
    8 RB

HQ 159 Inf Bde
    1 Cheshire/3 Mons
    4 KSLI
    1 Hereford
    2 Indep MG Coy (NF)

2. **6 AIRBORNE DIVISION**

RAC
    6 Airborne Armoured Recce Regt

HQ RA 6 Airborne Division
    6 Airldg Lt Regt RA
    6 Airldg A Tk Regt RA

HQ RE 6 Airborne Division
    3 Para Sqn RE
    591 Para Sqn RE
    249 Fd Coy RE
    286 Fd Pk Coy RE

HQ 3 Para Brigade
    8 Para Bn
    9 Para Bn
    Cdn Para Bn

HQ 5 Para Brigade
    7 Para Bn
    12 Para Bn
    13 Para Bn

HQ 6 Airldg Brigade
    1 RUR
    12 Devon
    52 Lt Inf (Ox & Bucks)

3. **15 (S) DIVISION**

   RAC
   15 (S) Recce Regt

   HQ RA 15 (S) Division
   131 Fd Regt RA
   181 Fd Regt RA
   190 Fd Regt RA
   102 A Tk Regt RA
   119 LAA Regt RA

   HQ RE 15 (S) Division
   20 Fd Coy RE
   278 Fd Coy RE
   279 Fd Coy RE
   624 Fd Pk Coy RE
   26 Br Pl RE

   HQ 44 (L) Brigade
   8 RS
   6 RSF
   6 KOSB

   HQ 46 (H) Brigade
   9 Cameronians
   7 Seaforth
   2 Glas H

   HQ 227 (H) Brigade
   10 HLI
   6 Seaforth
   2 A & SH

   MG Bn
   1 Mx

4. **5 INF DIVISION**
   RAC
       5 Recce Regt
   HQ RA 5 Inf Division
       91 Fd Regt RA
       92 Fd Regt RA
       156 Fd Regt RA
       52 A Tk Regt RA
       18 LAA Regt RA
   HQ RE 5 Inf Division
       245 Fd Coy RE
       252 Fd Coy RE
       38 Fd Coy RE
       254 Fd Pk Coy RE
   HQ 13 Brigade
       2 Cameronians
       2/5 Essex
       2 Wilts
   HQ 15 Brigade
       1 Green Howards
       1 KOYLI
       1 Y & L
   HQ 17 Brigade
       2 RSF
       2 Northamptons
       6 Seaforth
   MG Bn
       7 Cheshire

5. **6 GUARDS ARMOURED BRIGADE**
       4 Armd Gren Gds
       4 Armd Coldstream Guards
       3 Armd Scots Gds

6. **33 ARMOURED BRIGADE**
>   11 R Tks
>   One Sqn Staffs Yeo
>   77 Ass Sqn RE

7. **1 CDO BRIGADE**
>   3 Cdo
>   6 Cdo
>   45 (RM) Cdo
>   46 (RM) Cdo

8. **8 CORPS RA**
>   63 A tk Rgt RA
>   121 LAA Regt RA
>   10 Svy Regt RA

9. **8 AGRA**
>   25 Fd Regt RA
>   61 Med Regt RA
>   63 Med Regt RA
>   77 Med Regt RA
>   146 Med Regt RA
>   53 Hy Regt RA

10. **8 CORPS TPS RE**
>   100 Fd Coy RE
>   101 Fd Coy RE
>   224 Fd Coy RE
>   508 Fd Pk Coy RE

11. **11 AGRE**
>   **6 Army Tps Engrs**
>   69 Fd Coy RE
>   70 Fd Coy RE
>   183 Fd Coy RE
>   227 Fd Pk Coy RE
>   54 E & M Pl RE

7 Army Tps Engrs

    71 Fd Coy RE
    72 Fd Coy RE
    73 Fd Coy RE
    277 Fd Pk Coy RE
    19 E & M Pl RE

    279 Fd Coy RE
    81 Ass Sqn RE
    106 Br Coy RASC

ORDER OF BATTLE SUMMARISED

HQs Division:

    11 Armoured Division
    6 Airborne Division
    15 (S) Division
    5 Infantry Division

HQs RA:

    11 Armoured Division
    6 Airborne Division
    15 (S) Division
    5 Infantry Division
    8 AGRA

HQs RE:

    11 Armoured Division
    6 Airborne Division
    15 (S) Division
    5 Infantry Division
    11 AGRE

HQs Armoured Brigades:

      29 Armoured Bde
      6 Gds Armoured Bde
      33 Armoured Bde

HQs Infantry Brigades:

      159 Infantry Brigade
      3 Para Brigade
      5 Para Brigade
      6 Airldg Brigade
      44 (L) Brigade
      46 (H) Brigade
      227 (H) Brigade
      13 Brigade
      17 Brigade
      15 Brigade
      1 Commando Brigade

Armoured Units:

      Inns of Court
      Royals
      3 R Tks
      23 H
      15/19 H
      2 FF Yeo
      6 Airborne Armoured Recce Regt
      15 (S) Recce Regt
      5 Recce Regt
      4 Armoured Gren Gds
      4 Armoured Coldm Gds
      3 Armoured SG
      11 R Tks
      Sqn Staffs Yeo

RA Units:

13 RHA	156 Fd Regt
151 Fd Regt	52 A Tk Regt
65 A Tk Regt	18 LAA Regt
58 LAA Regt	25 Fd Regt
6 Airldg Lt Regt	61 Med Regt
6 Airldg A Tk Regt	63 Med Regt
131 Fd Regt	77 Med Regt
181 Fd Regt	146 Med Regt
190 Fd Regt	53 Hy Regt
102 A Tk Regt	63 Atk Regt RA
119 LAA Regt	121 LAA Regt RA
91 Fd Regt	10 Suy Regt RA
92 Fd Regt	

RE Units:

612 Fd Sqn RE	227 Fd Pk Coy RE
13 Fd Sqn RE	71 Fd Coy RE
147 Fd Pk Sqn RE	72 Fd Coy RE
3 Para Sqn RE	73 Fd Coy RE
591 Para Sqn RE	277 Fd Pk Coy RE
249 Fd Coy RE	279 Fd Coy RE
286 Fd Pk Coy RE	10 Br Pl RE
20 Fd Coy RE	26 Br Pl RE
278 Fd Coy RE	77 Assault Sqn RE
279 Fd Coy RE	81 Assault Sqn RE
624 Fd Pk Coy RE	91 E & M Pl RE
38 Fd Coy RE	8 Corps Tps RE
245 Fd Coy RE	106 Br Coy RASC
252 Fd Coy RE	100 Fd Coy RE
254 Fd Pk Coy RE	101 Fd Coy RE
69 Fd Coy RE	224 Fd Coy RE
70 Fd Coy RE	508 Fd Pk Coy RE
183 Fd Coy RE	

Infantry Units:

8 RB	6 KOSB
1 Cheshire	9 Cameronians
3 Mons	7 Seaforth
4 KSLI	2 Glas H
1 Hereford	10 HLI
2 Indep MG Coy (NF)	6 Seaforth
8 Para Bn	2 A & SH
9 Para Bn	1 Mx
Cdn Para Bn	2 Cameronians
7 Para Bn	2/5 Essex
12 Para Bn	2 Wilts
13 Para Bn	1 Green Howards
1 RUR	1 KOYLI
12 Devon	1 Y & L
52 Lt Inf	2 RSF
8 RS	2 Northamptons
6 RSF	6 Seaforth
3 Commando	6 Commando
	45 RM Commando
	46 RM Commando

HQ 8 CORPS

Commander	Lieutenant-General Sir Evelyn BARKER, KBE, CB, DSO, MC
BGS	Brigadier R. G. V. FITZGEORGE-BALFOUR, CBE, MC
GSO.1	Lt-Col J. G. HOOPER, OBE, 8H.
DA & QMG	Brigadier E. P. SEWELL, CBE
AQMG	Lt-Col A. B. COOTE, OBE, Northamptons
CCRA	Brigadier A. G. MATTHEW, DSO
CE	Brigadier H. H. C. SUGDEN, DSO, OBE
CSO	Brigadier W. R. SMIJTH-WINDHAM, DSO
DDST	Col W. H. BLACKIE, MC
DDMS	Brigadier J. MELVIN, OBE, MC, TD

ADH	Lt-Col A. M. MICHIE
DDOS	Col W. T. GRIMSDALE, OBE
DDME	Col M. A. W. McEVOY, OBE
APM	Lt-Col G. P. H. FITZGERALD, OBE, Foresters
SCAO/DDMG	Col G. H. PHIPPS-HORNBY
SO I Adm/ADMG (A)	Lt-Col R. S. MANLEY, Staffs Yeo
SO I Exec/ADMG (B)	Lt-Col A. W. E. CRAWFORD, Recce

8 CORPS TROOPS

The Royals	Lt-Col A. H. PEPYS, DSO
63 A Tk Regt	Lt-Col R. I. G. TAYLOR, DSO, MC
121 LAA Regt	Lt-Col R. H. L. BRACKENBURY
10 Svy Regt	Lt-Col E. A. SPENCER
CRE	Lt-Col J. E. MARSH
Comd R Sigs	Lt-Col R. C. CONWAY-GORDON
CRASC	Lt-Col G. C. W. NEVE
33 CCS	Lt-Col F. HEYWOOD-JONES, TD
34 CCS	Lt-Col R. EVANS
8 Corps Ord Field Park	Lt-Col W. ELLIOTT
ADOS	Lt-Col N. E. R. CARROLL
CREME	Lt-Col F. A. GOODMAN
812 (7) Armd Tps Wksps	Lt-Col R. H. ARBUCKLE
811 (Gds) Armd Tps Wksps	Lt-Col J. E. A. BELCHER
105 Corps Rec Camp	Lt-Col S. S. CAMERON
60 Pnr Gp	Lt-Col L. W. GILES, MC

COMMANDERS OF FORMATIONS and independent UNITS

— 5 Infantry Division	Major-General R. A. HULL, DSO
13 Brigade	Brigadier W. H. LAMBERT, CBE
15 Brigade	Brigadier C. HUXLEY, CBE
17 Brigade	Brigadier C. B. FAIRBANKS, MBE
CRA	Brigadier H. C. PHILIPPS, DSO
CRE	Lt-Col K. M. OSBORNE, DSO, MC
— 6 Airborne Division	Major-General E. L. BOLS, DSO
3 Parachute Brigade	Brigadier S. J. L. HILL, DSO, MC
5 Parachute Brigade	Brigadier J. H. N. POETT, DSO
6 Airlanding Brigade	Brigadier R. H. BELLAMY DSO,
	D/Commander Col. R. G. PARKER, DSO
CRA	Brigadier W. Mc. C. T. C. FAITHFULL
CRE	
— 11 Armoured Division	Major-General G.P.B. ROBERTS, CB, DSO, MC
29 Armoured Brigade	Brigadier C.B.C. HARVEY, DSO
159 Lorried Infantry Brigade	Brigadier J. B. CHURCHER, DSO
CRA	Brigadier B. J. FOWLER, DSO, MC
	Brigadier R. A. PHAYRE, DSO
CRE	Lt-Col G. L. GALLOWAY, DSO, GM
— 15 (S) Infantry Division	Major-General C. M. BARBER, CB, DSO
44 (L) Brigade	Brigadier Hon. H. C. T. CUMMING-BRUCE, DSO
46 (H) Brigade	Brigadier R. M. VILLIERS, DSO
227 (H) Brigade	Brigadier E. C. COLVILLE, DSO
CRA	Brigadier L. BOLTON, DSO
CRE	Lt-Col R. K. MILLAR, DSO

— 1 Commando Brigade	Brigadier D. MILLS-ROBERTS, DSO, MC
— 6 Guards Armoured Brigade	Brigadier W. D. GREENACRE, DSO, MVO
— 8 AGRA	Brigadier A. P. CAMPBELL, DSO, OBE
Two Squadrons SAS Regt	Lt-Col B. F. M. FRANKS, DSO, MC

DISTANCES OF MOVES OF HQ 8 CORPS
River RHINE to the BALTIC Sea

"WESEL TO LUBECK IN THIRTY SEVEN DAYS".

DATE	LOCATION	DISTANCE IN MILES
MAR 26	WESEL (R. RHINE)	
29	ERLE	14
30	KAPELLEN	21
31	LAER	17
APR 1	GREVEN	13
3	TECKLENBURG	18
4	BISSENDORF	20
5	HILLE	40
8	WOLPINGHAUSEN	26
11	NEGENBORN	25
13	CELLE AIRFIELD	18
14	HABIGHORST	13
16	HÖSSERINGEN	16
20	LUNEBURG (R. ELBE)	31
MAY 1	WANGELAU	20
2	LINAU	19
3	STOCKELSDORF (LUBECK)	26
39 DAYS	TOTAL ADVANCE	337 MILES

AVERAGE DAILY ADVANCE
RHINE to ELBE (Mar 27—Apr. 19) = 11⅛ miles
ELBE to BALTIC (Apr. 29—May 3) = 13 miles

The Terrain on 8 Corps axis from the RHINE to the BALTIC

1. **RIVER RHINE TO RIVER WESER.**

The greater part of the country between the RHINE and the WESER was a sandy plain. It was gently undulating farm country, like a richer form of Salisbury Plain. The soil was dry and provided good going; the few patches of peat bog were never so extensive that they could not be avoided. But across the plain lay on a belt of steep limestone hills, the TEUTOBURGERWALD; in front of these hills were two serious water obstacles, the River EMS and the DORTMUND-EMS Canal, and behind was a third, the MITTELLAND Canal.

The River EMS was the least of these obstacles: it was a meandering river, averaging 90 feet in width. Its approaches were fairly heavily wooded and it often had minor tributaries flowing close to it. In seizing the crossing at GREVEN in the dark, one of these tributaries was mistaken for the main stream, which unfortunately resulted in the bridge being blown before it could be captured.

The DORTMUND - EMS Canal was close to and parallel with the EMS River. The canal was about 110 feet wide, with steep grass and stone banks. Within the Corps boundaries were five existing crossing sites (places with reasonably good road approaches). Of these, the Northern two were within 2000 yards of the high ridge of the TEUTOBURGERWALD, which completely dominated them. At the centre crossing place Bomber Command had obliterated the canal and the approaches to it; only a desolate marsh, pitted with huge craters, remained. The next site had also suffered from heavy bombing, and although the canal itself was dry, the approaches were badly damaged. The Southern crossing, which was eventually used as the Corps axis, had a good bridging site. But the road on the far side went in a South-Westerly direction, and in order to regain the road to LENGERICH the axis had to use a couple of rough unmade tracks; after a few hours of traffic both of these had disintegrated at several places, and had to have major engineer repairs.

The TEUTOBURGERWALD consisted of a series of steep and thickly wooded ridges, at right angles to the Corps axis. The first ridge was broken by only three narrow defiles, and the new good roads twisted through these defiles, enclosed by the thick woods. A more ideal defensive position could not exist. The country between the ridges was open farmland, which at first sight looked good normal ground; but it was soft wet clay, over which no tank or truck could go, so that all traffic had to keep to the roads.

The MITTELLAND Canal varied in width between 100 and 130 feet, and had steep grass banks about ten feet high. A branch Canal ran South East from the main canal to OSNABRUCK, and this also had to be crossed by 11th Armoured Division.

Roads available to the Corps were never of high class. During the first thirty miles metalled roads were rare, and the Corps had to rely on sandy tracks for much of its routes. COESFELD, a focus of many roads between the RHINE and EMS, had been bombed thoroughly a few days before our arrival, and no way was left through the town. After COESFELD there were plenty of roads, but either the surface was poor, or they were narrow or twisting. In the clay valleys of the TEUTOBURGERWALD, where tanks were forced to use the roads, the verges crumbled rapidly under the strain and deep muddy ruts formed beside the road; therefore only one way traffic was possible by day, and at night a small slip caused vehicles to become bogged or sometimes to turn over.

2. **RIVER WESER TO RIVER ELBE.**

The WESER was between 250 and 300 feet wide within the Corps boundaries and at the beginning of April the current in the river was flowing fairly fast. The East bank consisted of clay meadows, which were almost devoid of trees, hedges or any other form of cover. To add to the difficulties, a new canal was under construction at PETERSHAGEN, where the Corps axis crossed the river; this canal consisted of a deep cutting partly filled with water, 250 to 700 yards back from the river.

Beyond the WESER, all the way to the ELBE, the sandy plains continued. Woods were common, and some long stretches of forest were encountered (e. g. between CELLE and UELZEN, where the axis passed through 16 miles of continuous forest).

There were two further water obstacles, the Rivers LEINE and ALLER. The LEINE was a small river, 60 to 100 feet wide, with relatively dry ground on both banks. The ALLER was wider and more difficult: at 11th Armoured Division's crossing site the far bank consisted of a narrow wooded ridge, beyond which was an impassable marsh; 15 (Scottish) Division crossed in the town of CELLE, where the river had two courses, running between stone walls and houses.

Between the WESER and the ALLER the roads had the same defects as before the WESER, either they had poorly made surfaces, or they were narrow or twisting. After the ALLER they were better — a first class "Reichstrasse" went from CELLE to UELZEN and LUNEBURG, which at first was partially blocked by demolitions, but was repaired within a few days.

3. RIVER ELBE TO THE BALTIC.

The ELBE at LAUENBURG was almost as wide as the RHINE at WESEL — about 1100 feet. The South bank consisted of flat marshland, divided from the river by a high flood dyke. In contrast, the North bank was a steep escarpment about 100 feet high: at the town the streets and houses were built up the escarpment, while West of the town the slope was covered by scrub. This escarpment dominated the South bank of the river, and the Germans were able to observe any movement on our side by day. But once this feature had been captured, it acted as a good protection to the bridging sites, since it made them immune from any ground observation.

Between the ELBE and the BALTIC were two distinct types of country. For the first fifteen miles there was the same sandy plain as all the way from the Rhine. Then the ground became more hilly, with numerous small rounded hummocks, and irregular little valleys sometimes filled by lakes. In addition between the fields were earth banks, with tough tree hedges growing out of them; in type they were the same as the hedges of Normandy "bocage". In fact, the country became very picturesque, though tiresome and difficult for cross country movement. By this time the enemy opposition was such that terrain was of little importance.

Operation "ENTERPRISE"

1. Details are shown below of the numbers and types of guns which were available for Operation "Enterprise" together with some details of the actual expenditure of ammunition during the Assault Crossing.

Type of Gun	Number	Expenditure of Ammunition Estimated	Rounds fired per gun
3.7 How	24		
75 mm Pack How	24		
25 pr	240	232	222
5.5" Med	48	169	150
4.5" Med	16	159	172
155 mm	24	58	68
7.2"	24	72	54
3.7" AA	24		

2. The following bridging agents were available for the Assault Crossing.

	Estimated Time of Completion	Actual Time
LVT ferry	H hour D day	0200 hrs 29 Apr
Cl 9 Raft	H + 11 hours	1300 hrs 29 Apr
Cl 40 Raft	H + 12 hours	1410 hrs 29 Apr
	H + 14 hours	1600 hrs 29 Apr

Cl 9 Br	H + 18 hours	2015 hrs 29 Apr
Cl 40 Br	H + 34 hours	1200 hrs 30 Apr

Bridging was continually delayed by enemy action. A total of 12324 vehicles crossed the River Elbe over the two bridges alone between 29 April and 2 May inclusive.

H hour was 0200 hrs 29 April

Formation or Unit	Number of vevicles
11 Armd Div	1590
5 Brit Div	2921
15 (S) Div including a Brigade of 53 Div	2775
6 Airborne Div	3458
8 Corps Main HQ	218
Greys (one Sqn.)	130
Royals	220
8 Corps Tps RE	180
6 Gds Armd Bde	400
Other Corps Tps	432

This excludes Vehicles taken across by LVT ferry and rafts which were used entirely by 15 (S) Division and 1 Commando Brigade.

BRIDGES BUILT BY 8 CORPS FROM RHINE TO BALTIC

Serial	Date	Army Dump	Corps Dump	Location	Bridge Built	Bridge Strengthened	Formation	Tonnage of approximate equipment
1	March 26—27	GOCH	SONNSBECK & WESEL	R. LIPPE A. 247390	Bailey Pontoon Class 40		8 Corps Troops RE	170
2	28			A. 253437	Bailey 60 Feet, Class 40		8 Corps Troops RE	30
3	28			A. 292474	Bailey 80 Feet, Class 40		8 Corps Troops RE	40
4	29—30			A. 549626	Bailey 60 Feet, Class 40		8 Corps Troops RE	30
5	30			A. 441665	Bailey 40 Feet, Class 40		8 Corps Troops RE	15
6	30		VELEN A. 4868	A. 570630	Bailey 50 Feet, Class 40		16 Airfield Construction Group	30
7	31		ALTENBERGE A. 826839	V. 842041	Bailey 100 Feet, Class 40		11 Armoured Division	42
8	31			GREVEN A. 908884	Bailey 110 Feet, Class 40		8 Corps Troops RE	45
9	31			A. 911885	Bailey 110 Feet, Class 40		6 Airborne Division RE	45
10	Apr 1			EMSDETTEN A. 868968	Bailey 110 Feet, Class 40		8 Corps Troops RE	45
11	1—2			DORENTHE V. 960026 DORTMUND-EMS-CANAL	Bailey Pontoon 190 Feet, Class 40		8 Corps Troops RE	120
12	1			A. 977892 DORTMUND-EMS-CANAL V. 953052	Bailey 120 Feet, Class 40		6 Airborne Division RE	55
13	1				Bailey 120 Feet, Class 40		11 Armoured Division	55
14	5	BURGSTEINFURT A.7294	OSNABRUCK & HILLE W 6817	STOLZENAU W. 915356 Br abandoned owing enemy action	Bailey Pontoon 240 Feet, Class 40		11 Armoured Division RE	160

		Date	Location	Bridge	Notes	Unit	
15		April 6	PETERSHAGEN W. 8318 R WESER	FBE 200 Feet, Class 9		6 Airborne Division RE	45
16		6—7	W. 8329 R WESER	Bailey Pontoon 320 Feet, Class 40		8 Corps Troops RE	250
17	WOLFELEHDE (No. 6) X. 1844	8	SCHLUSSELBURG W. 918322 R WESER	Bailey Pontoon Class 40		15 (S) Division RE & 8 Corps Troops RE	180
18		9	NEUSTADT X. 176358 R LEINE	Bailey 50 Feet, Class 40		6 Airborne Division RE	?
19		10—11	HELSTORF X. 252452 R LEINE	Bailey 170 Feet, Class 40		11 Armoured Division RE	100
20		12	ESSEL X. 300576 R ALLER	Bailey 150 Feet, Class 40		11 Armoured Division RE	85
21		12	CELLE X. 590505	Bailey 30 Feet, Class 40		15 (S) Division RE	20
22		12	—do—	Bailey 90 Feet, Class 40		15 (S) Division RE	40
23		13	WIETZE X. 422535	Bailey 30 Feet, Class 40		8 Corps Troops RE	?
24		13—14	X. 667604	Bailey 60 Feet, Class 40		15 (S) Division RE	25
25		14	X. 503555	Bailey 40 Feet, Class 18		11 Armoured Division RE	15
26		15—16	X. 8070	Bailey 30 Feet, Class 40		11 Armoured Division RE	20
27		15—16	WINSEN X. 4756	Bailey 160 Feet, Class 40		6 Airborne Troops RE	90
28	SUDERBURG (No. 7) X. 8280	15	X. 785701	Bailey 60 Feet, Class 40		15 (S) Division RE	24
29		16	X. 602783	Bailey 80 Feet, Class 40		11 Armoured Division RE	35
30	SULINGEN	16	X. 906852	Bailey 50 Feet, Class 40	Br str to Cl 12	15 (S) Division RE	18
31		17	X. 878803		Widened	6 Airborne Division RE	—

BRIDGES BUILT 8 CORPS FROM RHINE TO BALTIC

Serial	Date	Army Dump	Corps Dump	Location	Bridge Built	Bridge Strengthened	Formation	Tonnage of approximate equipment
32	April 17			X. 898713		Str to Cl 12	6 Airborne Division RE	—
33	18			UELZEN X. 920887	Timber 20 Feet, Class 18		5 Division RE	—
34	18			X. 670730		Timber bridge strengthened to Class 12	11 Armoured Division RE	—
35	19			S. 728300	Bailey 70 Feet, Class 40		11 Armoured Division RE	30
36	19			S. 786163	Bailey 70 Feet, Class 40		11 Armoured Division RE	30
37	19			UELZEN X. 920877	Timber Class 40		15 (S) Division RE	—
38	19			LUNEBURG S. 800226	Bailey 40 Feet, Class 40		11 Armoured Division RE	20
39	20			S. 804285	Bailey 50 Feet, Class 24		11 Armoured Division	25
40	20		No. 8 DUMP S. 892311	S. 813319	Bailey 60 Feet, Class 40		11 Armoured Division RE	25
41	20			S. 822324	Bailey 40 Feet, Class 40		11 Armoured Division	20
42	20			S. 778178		Widening existing br	8 Corps Troops RE	—
43	20—24			S. 785163	Bailey 70 Feet, Class 70 Doubling up Ser 35		8 Corps Troops RE	45
44	20			S. 847271	Bailey 60 Feet, Class 40 (two-way)		6 Airborne Troops RE & 15 (S) Division RE	50
45	20			S. 895315		Existing bridge strengthened to Class 40	11 Armoured Division RE	—
46	21			Y. 012948	Timber Class 9		5 Division RE	—
47	21—28			Y. 012950	Timber Class 40 (two-way).		5 Division RE	—

#	Date	Location	Bridge	Notes	Unit	Tonnage
48	Apr 21		S. 849271	Bailey 60 Feet, Class 40		6 Airborne Troops RE	25
49	21		S. 803285	Bailey 50 Feet, Class 40		8 Corps Troops RE	25
50	22—27		S. 780322	Doubling up Ser 38 Timber 50 Feet, Class 40		15 (S) Division RE	25
51	24		X. 906907		Bridge strengthened to Class 40	8 Corps Troops RE	—
52	24—25		S. 879293	Timber Class 9	Bridge strengthened to Class 40	5 Infantry Division RE	—
53	25		S. 952182		—do—	6 Airborne Troops RE	—
54	25		S. 951189			6 Airborne Troops RE	—
55	26	DOHREN S. 3123	S. 983183	Timber Cl 40		5 Division RE	—
56	26—27		S. 644166	Imp Class 40		11 Armoured Division RE	30
57	26—27		S. 813318	Bailey 80 Feet, Class 40	Class 9 Bridge strengthened to Class 40	15 (S) Division RE	—
58	26—27		S. 646166		Bridge strengthened to Class 70	?	—
59	28		Y. 012980	Timber Class 40		5 Division RE	—
60	26		S. 948271 (?)	Timber Class 40		?	—
61	28		S. 641289			?	—
62	29		R ELBE LAUENBURG	FBE 920 Feet, Class 9		8 Corps Troops RE	220
63	29—30		R ELBE ARTLENBURG	Bailey Pontoon 870 Feet, Class 40		11 Airborne Group RE	650
64	May 1		S. 846516	Bailey 50 Feet, Class 40		?	25
65	1		S. 878424	Bailey 60 Feet, Class 40		15 (S) Division RE	20
66	1		S. 920568	Bailey 60 Feet, Class 40		?	25
					APPROXIMATE TOTAL TONNAGE EQUIPMENT	3000

Thus the Corps, during the whole of this period, erected

1120 feet of Class 9 Bridge,
60 feet of Class 18 Bridge,
50 feet of Class 24 Bridge,
2430 feet of Class 40 Bridge,
1620 feet of Class 40 Bailey Pontoon Bridge,
and 70 feet of Class 70 Bridge.

Notes on Bridge Classification

The Class 9 Bridge will take a loaded 3 ton lorry, the TETRARCH Light Tank, Scout Cars, and Carriers of all types.

The Class 18 Bridge takes in Addition, all light tanks, Armoured Cars, and Armoured Command vehicles.

The Class 40 Bridge takes all tanks up to and including the Churchill, and the selfpropelled 25 Pounder Gun, and 17 Pounder Anti-Tank Guns.

The Class 70 Bridge will take anything up to a loaded Tank Transporter.

Story of the RASC after the RHINE crossing

58 FMC was established North East of WESEL as soon as the initial priority convoys had crossed the RHINE. To ensure a quick turn-round on the bridges, an ammunition build-up of approximately six 3-ton platoons of Gun ammunition and one 3-ton platoon mixed was dumped at ISSUM. Later Compo rations were added to this dump.

On the word 'go' ammunition was rushed over the RHINE, and the daily maintenance pack was diverted through from 57 FMC to 58 FMC. An additional 10 platoons of transport was placed under commando of 8 Corps to make the Airborne Division and Commando Brigade fully mobile. 3 platoons were very late in reporting due to congestion on the bridges and the fact that the Army due to congestion on the bridges and the fact that the Army road head was moving across the RHINE to the BOCHOLT area. This transport was used to bring up additional POL and Supplies from 8 Army Road Head to 58 FMC before going on and reporting. In all approximately 2500 tons of ammunition, 250 Supplies, 500 tons POL and Engineer stores was put into this FMC.

However, it became necessary to move 58 FMC further North to enable the Americans to take over the area just

South of WESEL. 36 hours were allowed for this move. All available transport was thrown into this, including 1st line unit transport and an additional lift was given by DUKWS from Airborne resources. Only 500 tons of ammunition was left in 59 FMC; all other stocks had successfully been cleared to 59 FMC at RHEDE, near BOCHOLT in the following priority (1) POL (2) Supplies (3) ammunition. Stores left behind were frozen in the American zone.

The Army transport on loan was then handed over to 6 Airborne Division and the Commando Brigade. Each vehicle tied 36 Jerricans on the outside and 12 Compo packs inside, so that if road communications were cut on the advance, a reserve would be available.

60 FMC was opened at VELEN near COESFELD, but it was a short lived affair as the speed of the advance had increased. FMC stocks were moved forward mostly by 3rd line, but Formation transport dumped its loads in the new FMC locations, then reloaded from the old FMC, and returned to Company location.

Part of the transport on loan to 6 Airborne Division was switched to help 15 (S) Division move forward. 5 Para Brigade was also ordered forward and transport resources were again stretched to carry this out.

The daily pack of approx 100,000 rations, 100,000 MT80 and 90 tons ammunition were brought up daily, in some cases transport taking 2 days to do the turn-round.

61 FMC was opened at BISSENDORF, South East of OSNABRUCK, after many delays, DDST and Brigadier A/Q taking some prisoners who tried to hold them up whilst on the FMC recconaissance. Whilst the stocking of the FMC was going on, one Platoon Commander was shot up by some stray Wehrmacht.

Army Road Head had by now moved up to RHINE, and CRASC 44 Transport Column was established in that area, and given the task of loading the daily pack and dispatching forward.

When 62 FMC opened at HILLE near LUBBECKE the distance to the Army Road Head was over 100 miles making a 2 to 3 day turn-round including loading and unloading. All empty transport returning to Road Head was used to take back prisoners. Convoys coming up also brought reinforcements.

63 FMC was established and built up very quickly at NEUSTADT, which proved a very useful and well laid out FMC. Stocks from 61 FMC which had not been cleared were brought direct here. Rear parties had been left behind at all FMC's and issues were made to formations with sufficient transport to collect. There was never sufficient labour or transport to clear the FMCs direct, and at one time there were 3 FMCs in operation, as well as normal drawings at Army Road Head, now moved to UCHTE.

Captured stocks were getting increasingly difficult to guard, but full use was made of vast quantities of frozen or tinned vegetables and meat found in STEINHUDE. These were later handed over to Military Government.

The advance continued, and 64 FMC was established in CELLE. It was intended to stock only Supplies and POL here, and to continue ammunition at 63. Later it was decided to stock all three commodities at 64, as the tonnage lifts of ammunition were again on the increase and a gradual build-up for the Elbe crossing was in progress.

At the same time, the infamous BELSEN CAMP was made an 8 Corps responsibility and Supplies and transport were despatched to the Camp, the Supplies in the Camp being organised by the Camp Platoon of 22 Coy RASC. Captured stocks from CELLE and STEINHUDE were used as initial supplies to BELSEN and later surplus American C Packs were taken in

The war moved forward, and LUNEBURG was chosen as 65 FMC. Stocks were moved by transport from 64 FMC, and REME made trains work between CELLE and BIENENBUTTEL, transport completing the job from there to LUNEBURG, some 12 miles distant. The trains arrived each morning and consisted of 26 10 ton trucks. Transport from Corps Head Quarters and local units was used on the clearing of these trains.

Meanwhile LUNEBURG was built up to the largest stocks held in any previous FMC, and it was not until after it had been operating for 6 to 7 days that stocks of previous FMCs caught up. Just before the ELBE crossing, Army took over 65 FMC as a basis for their new Army Road Head, but Formations were still based on this FMC for maintenance.

66 FMC at LUBECK was the final FMC and only closed down when NEUMUNSTER was made 8 Corps District Maintenance Centre.

137 and 122 DIDs were the two Supply units with the Corps all through this operation with the Composite Platoon of 22 Company standing in when there were three FMCs to be looked after. 230 Petrol Depot worked with all FMCs splitting up as necessary, and occasionally helped by a Platoon of 35 Company. HQ CRASC 44 Transport Column was looked upon as belonging to 8 Corps, and during the time it was under command many and various companies were under its command. Field Bakeries were a great asset to the Corps in the supply of fresh bread, about which very few complaints were ever heard.

Divisional CsRASC were always very helpful in the supply of transport, and appreciated that whenever transport was requested by Corps, there was a job to do. Transport was always very scarce, but it is thought that there was never an occasion when the RASC were not able to respond.

1. 6 A/B Div crossing site of the R. Ems at Greven.

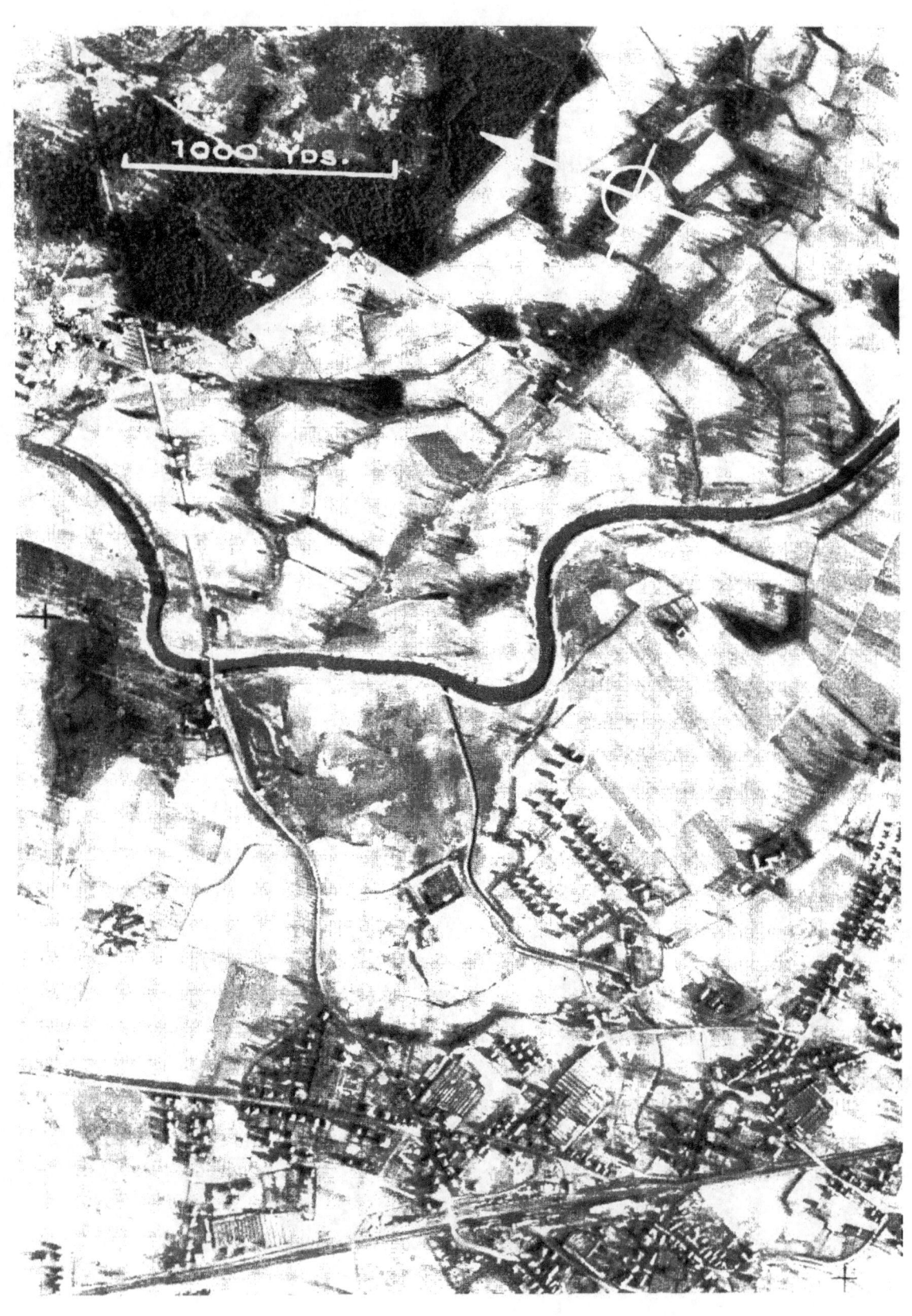

2. 11 Armd Div crossing site of the R. Ems, East of Emsdetten.

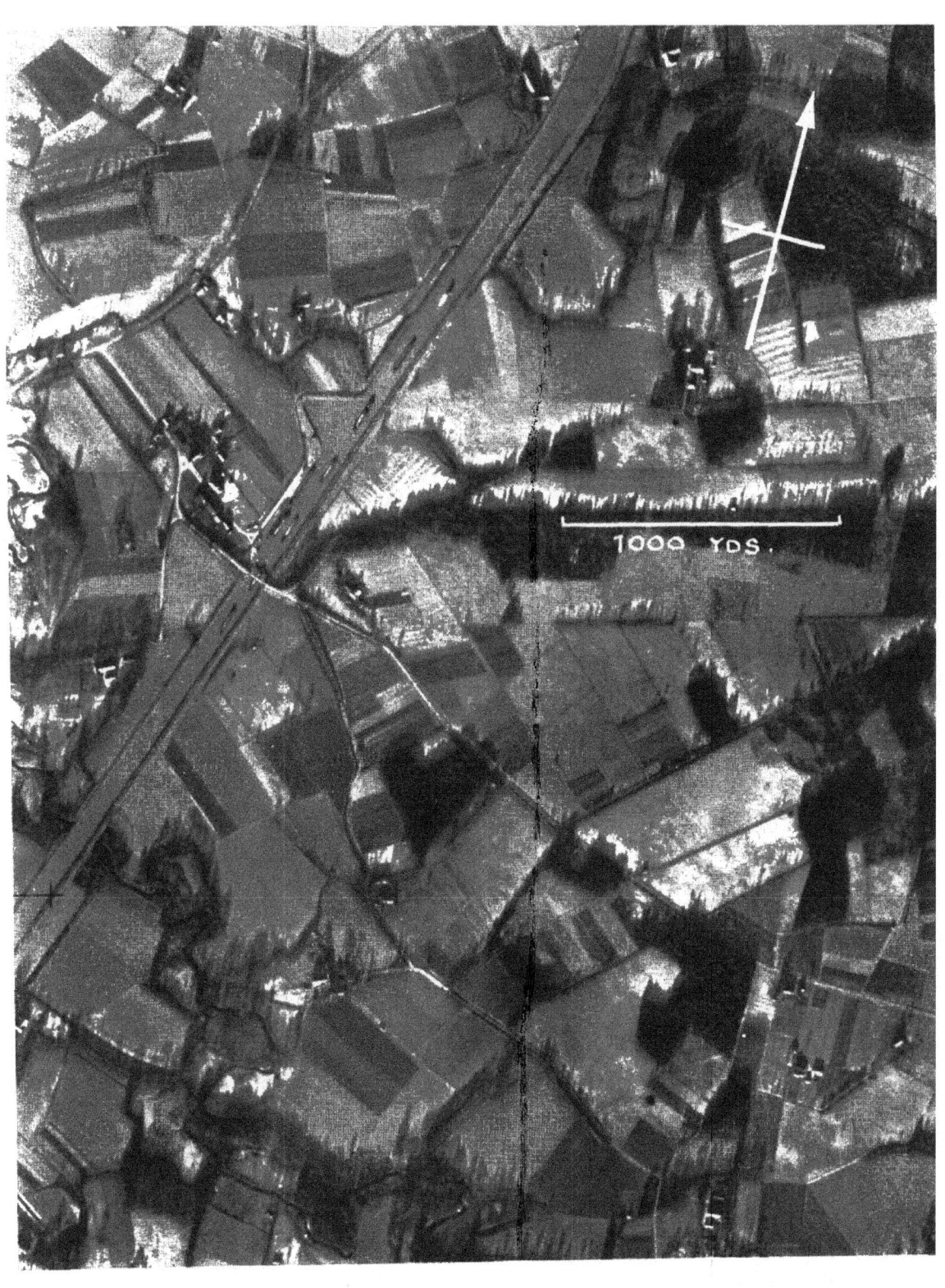

3. 6 A/B Div crossing site of the Dortmund-Ems-Canal.

4 11 Armd Div crossing site of the Dortmund-Ems-Canal.

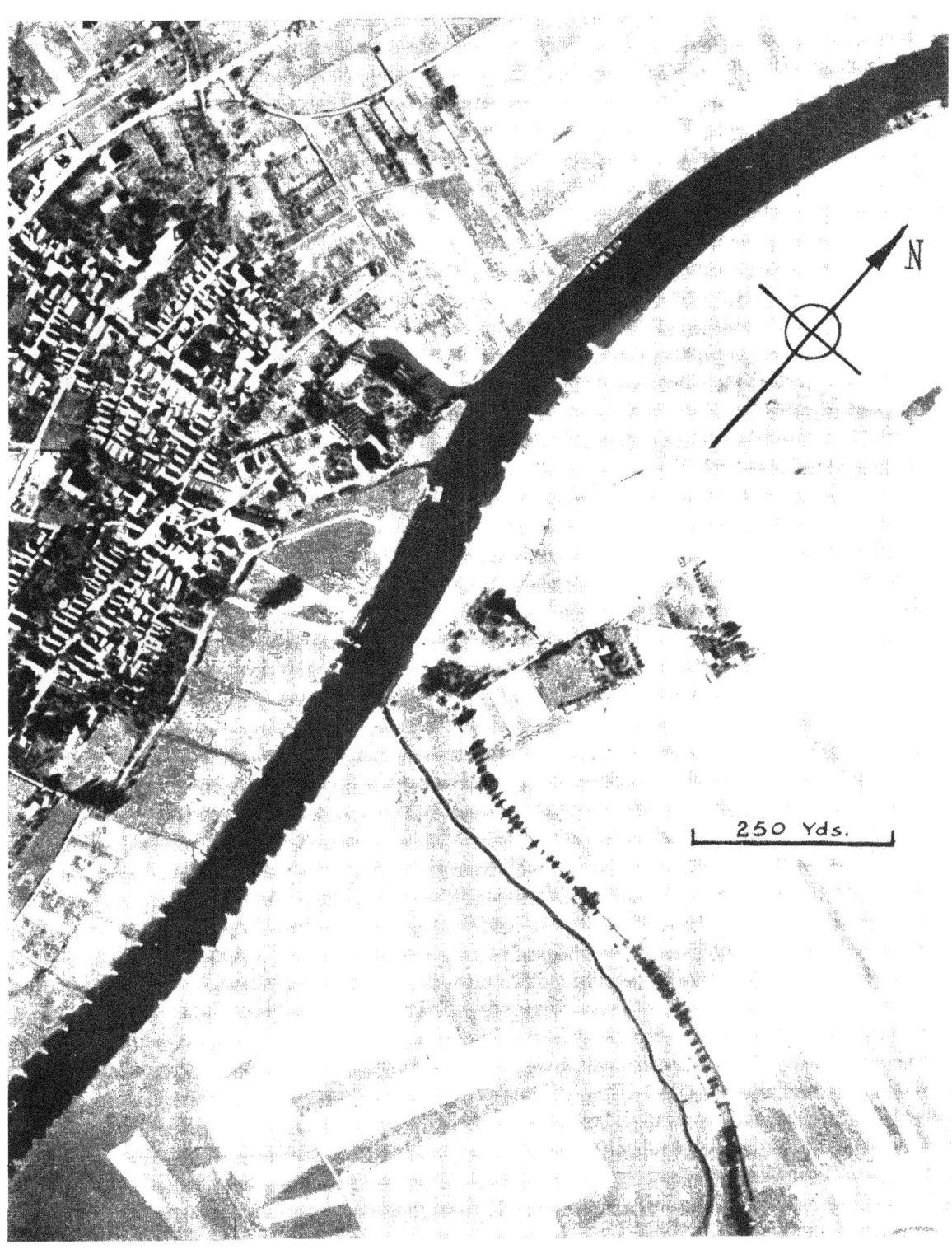

5. Corps axis crossing point of the R. Weser at Petershagen.
This photograph was taken six months after the operation.

6. 11 Armd Div's original crossing site of the R. Weser at Stolzenau.
This had to be abandoned owing to enemy air action.

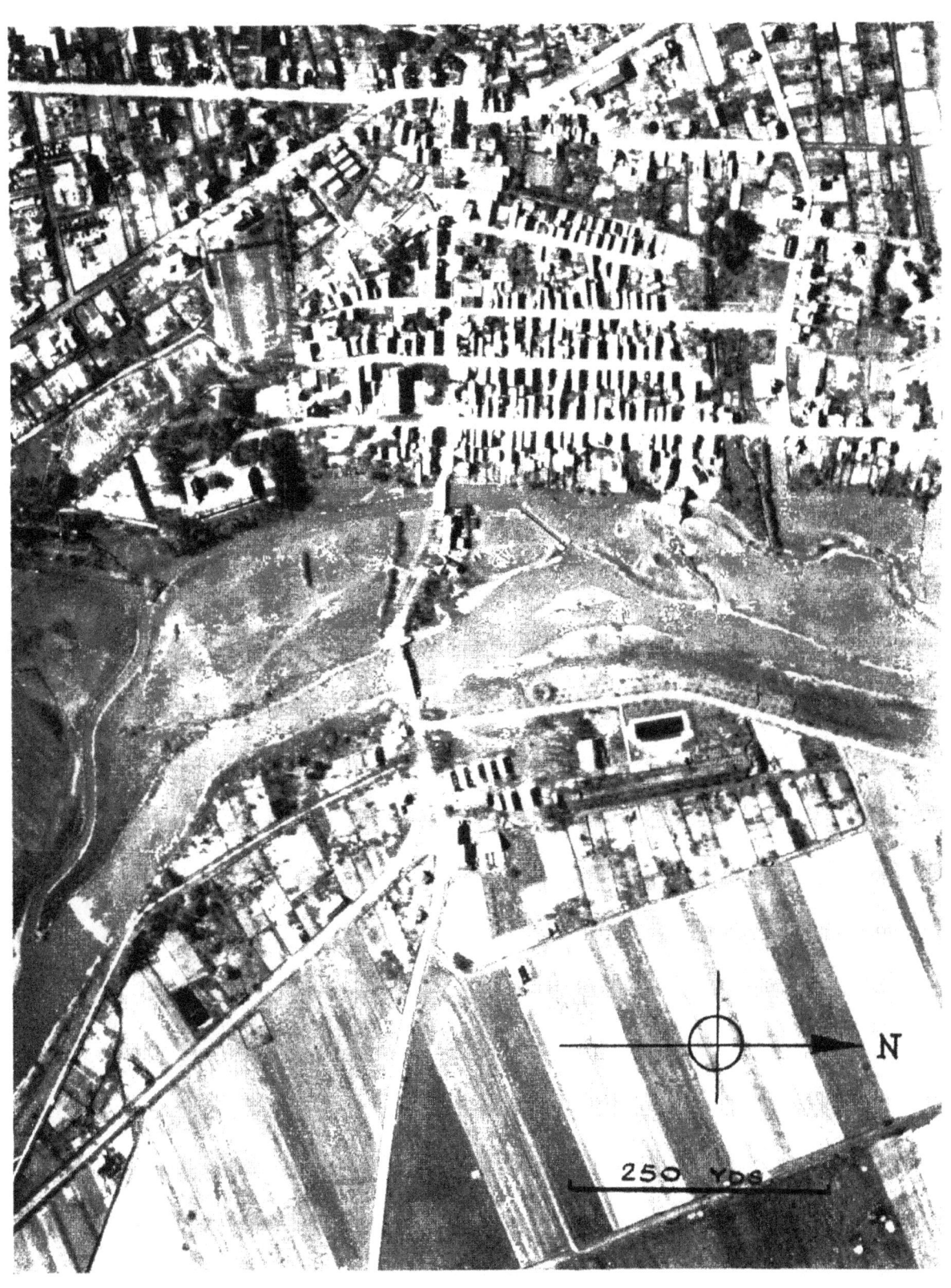

7. The R. Leine at Neustadt, where it was crossed by 6 A/B and 15 (S) Divs.

2. The R. Leine at Helstorf, where it was crossed by 11 Armd Div.

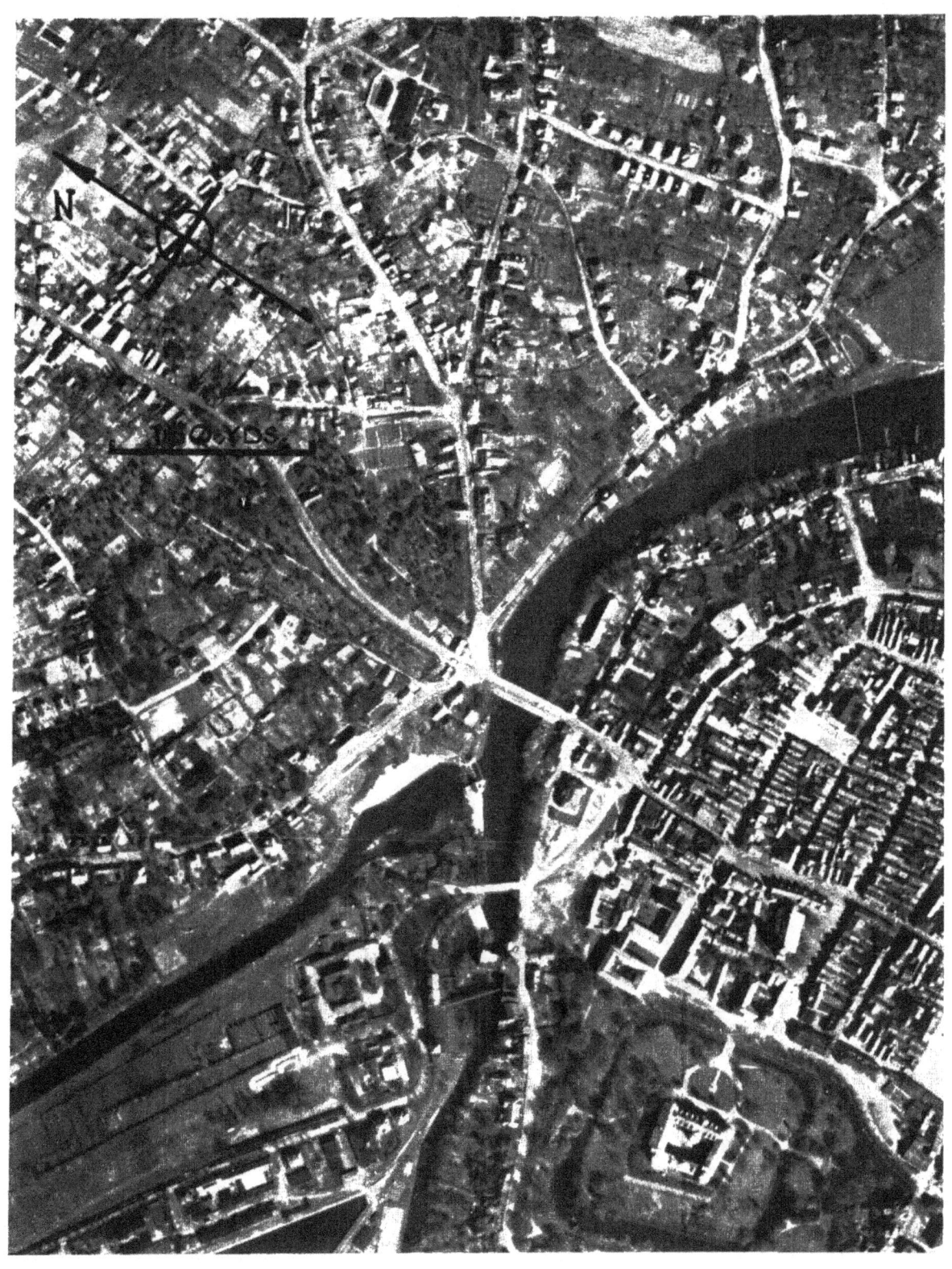

9. Celle, showing the crossing site of the R. Aller used by 15 (S) Div.

10 The railway bridge over the R. Aller near Essel at which 11 Armd Div made the first crossing of the river.

11. The road bridge over the R. Aller, NE of Essel. This picture was taken the day before the enemy destroyed the bridge. 11 Armd Div subsequently constructed a new bridge here.

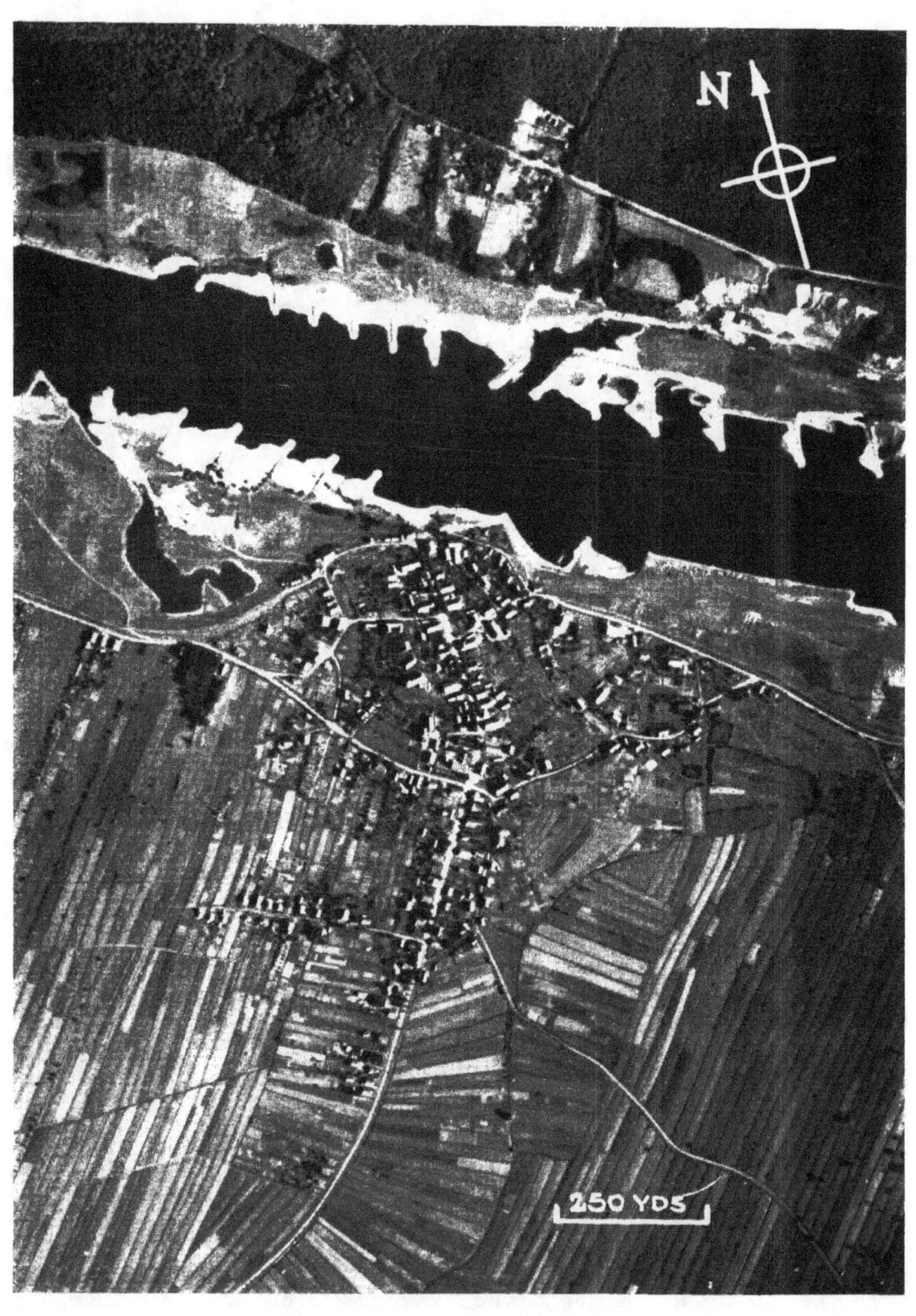

12. The R. Elbe at Artlenburg, where the 15 (S) Div crossing was made.

13. The R. Elbe at Lauenburg, where 1 Cdo Bde crossed.
This picture was taken three days before the crossing,
and shows the demolished road/railway bridge.

WESER

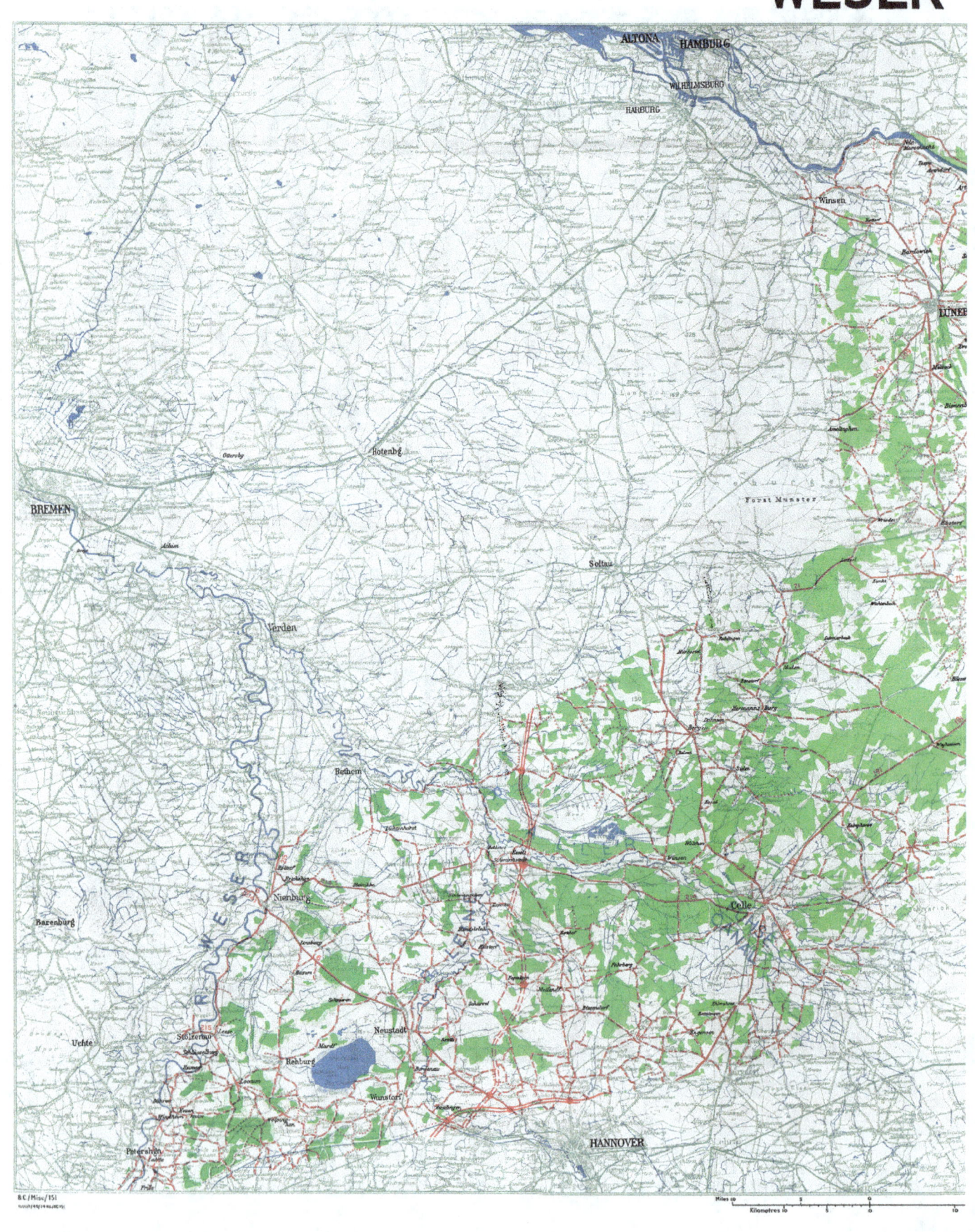

TO ELBE

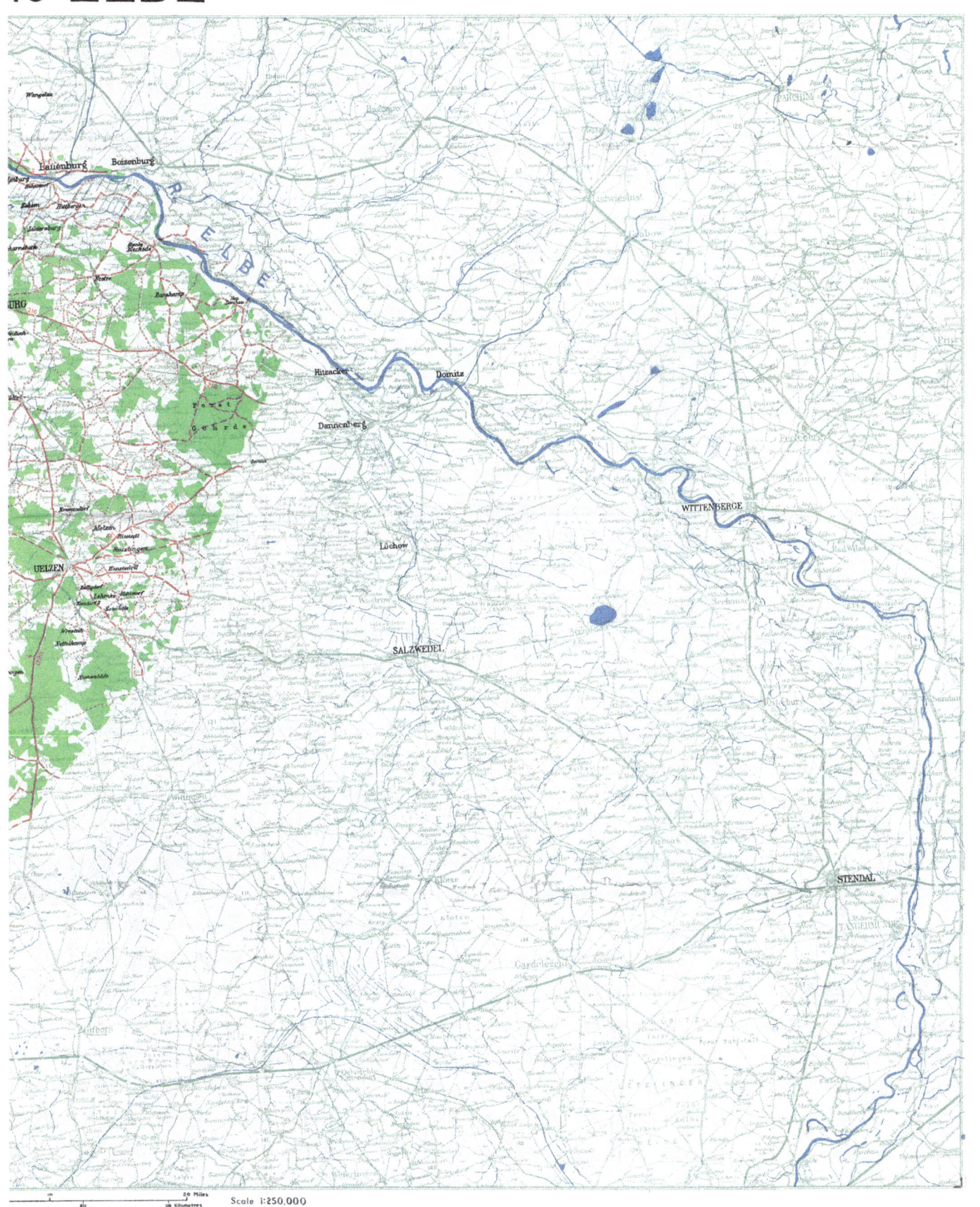

WESER TO ELBE

SPREAD 1	SPREAD 2	SPREAD 3
SPREAD 4	SPREAD 5	SPREAD 6
SPREAD 7	SPREAD 8	SPREAD 9

SPREAD 1

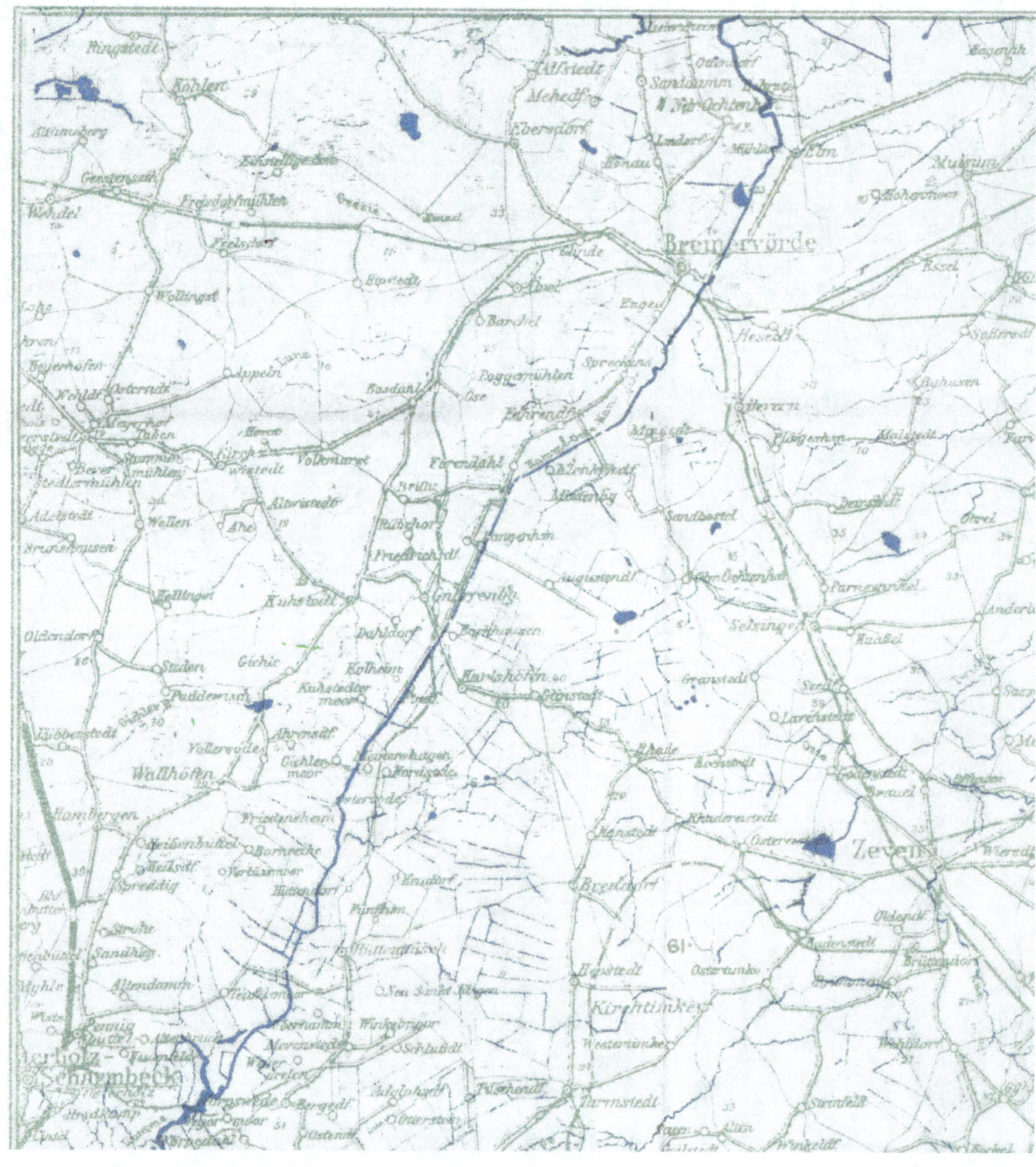

SPREAD 1

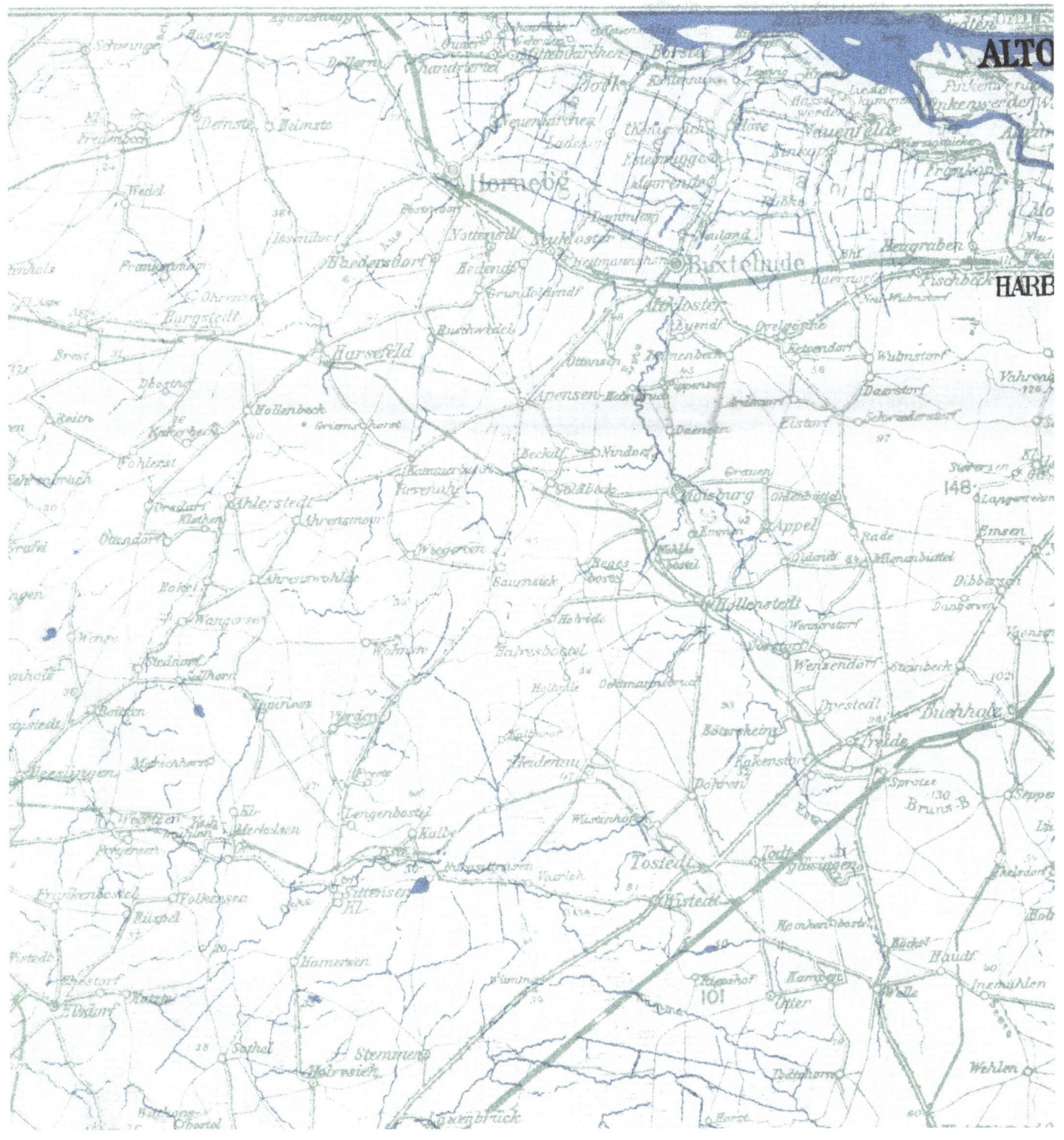

WESER

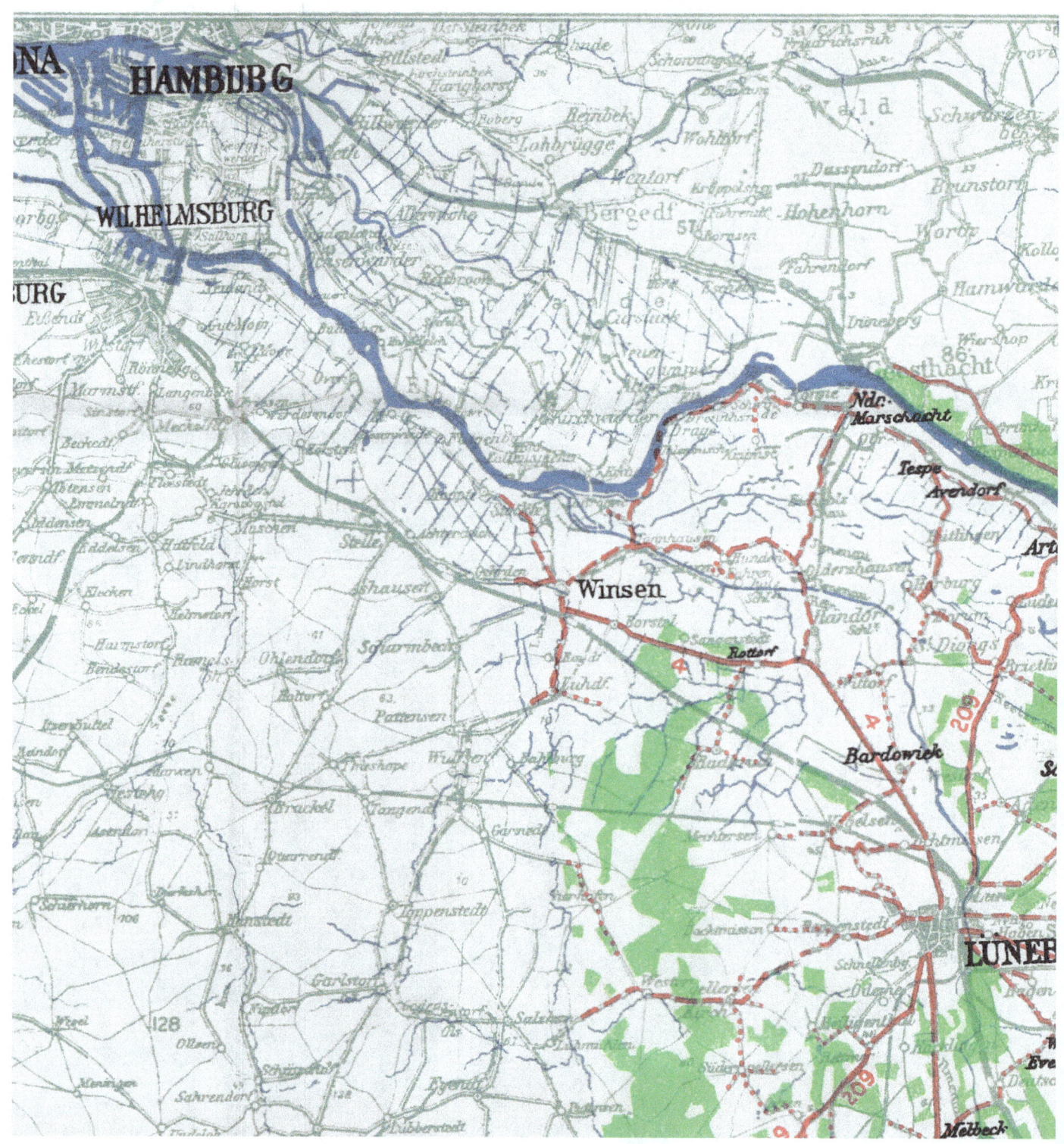

TO ELBE

SPREAD 3

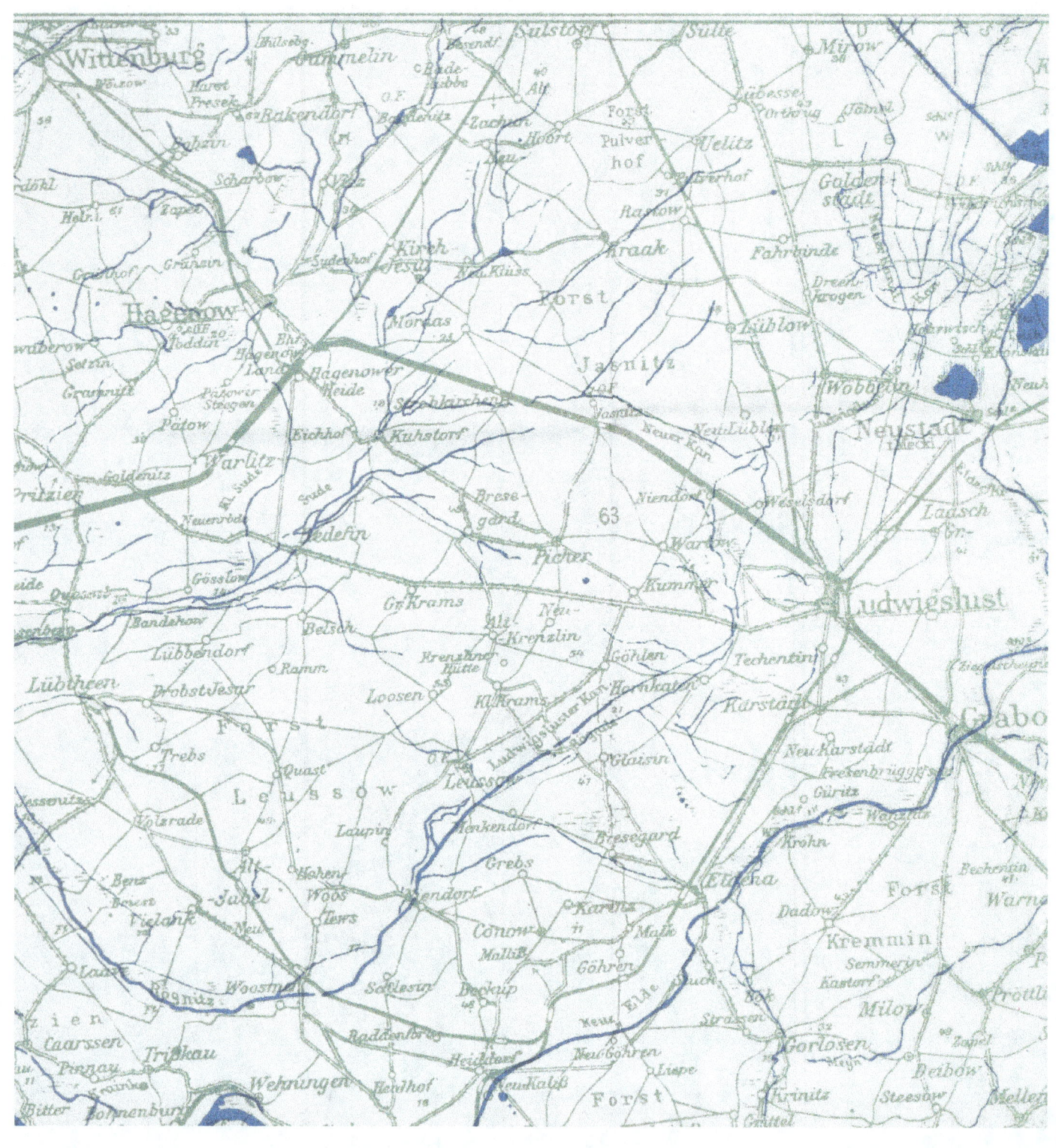

SPREAD 3

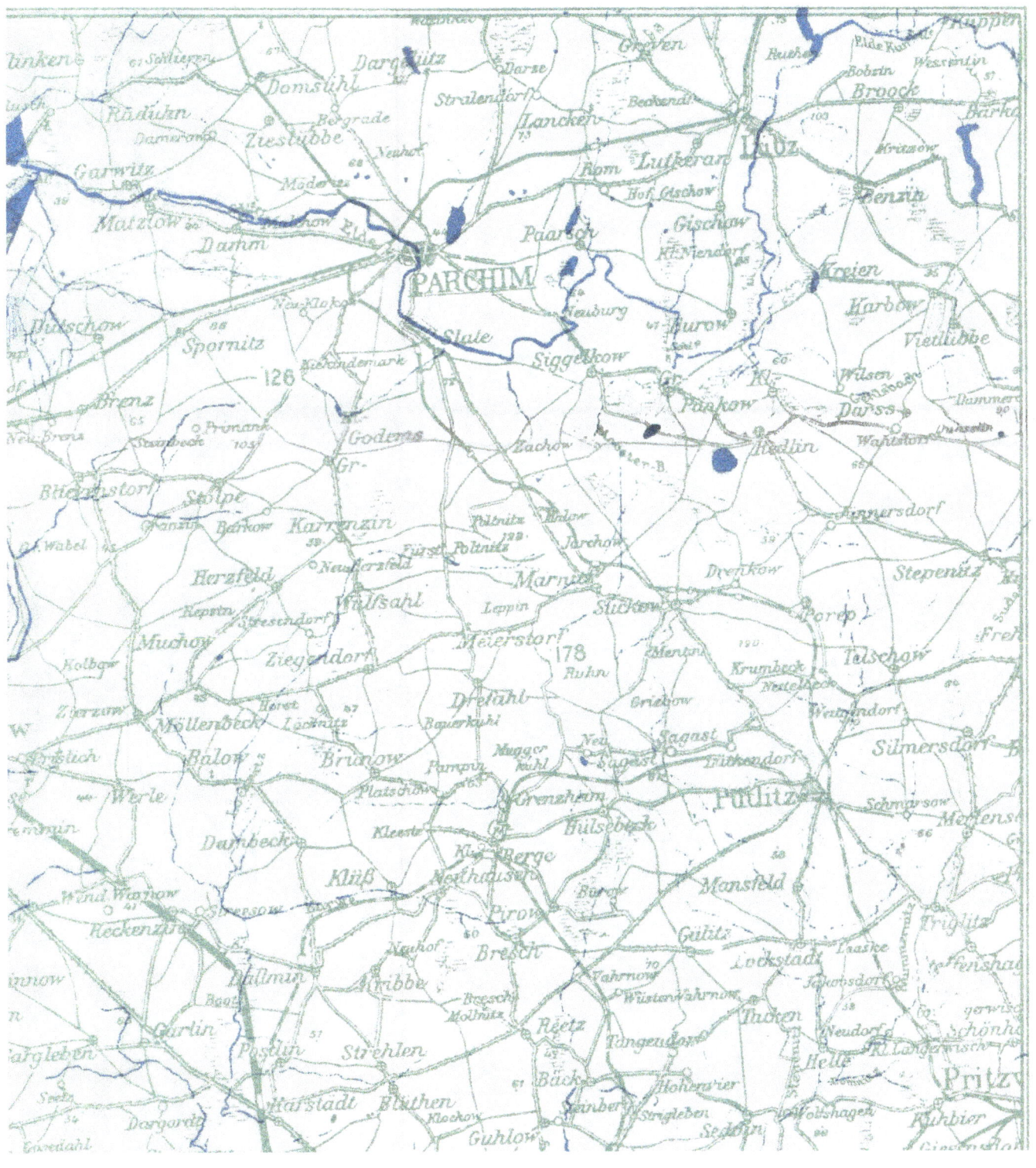

SPREAD 4

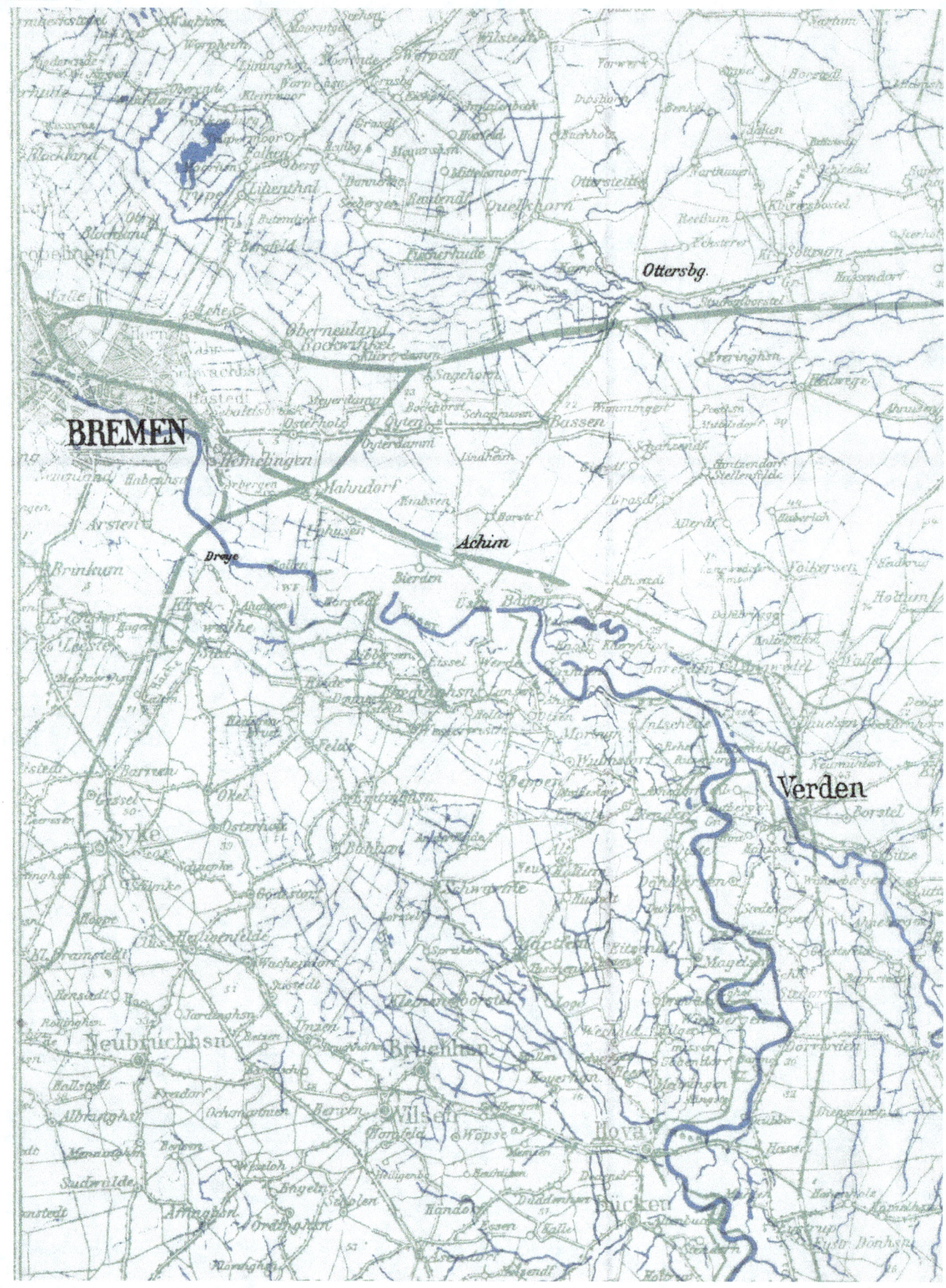

SPREAD 4

SPREAD 5

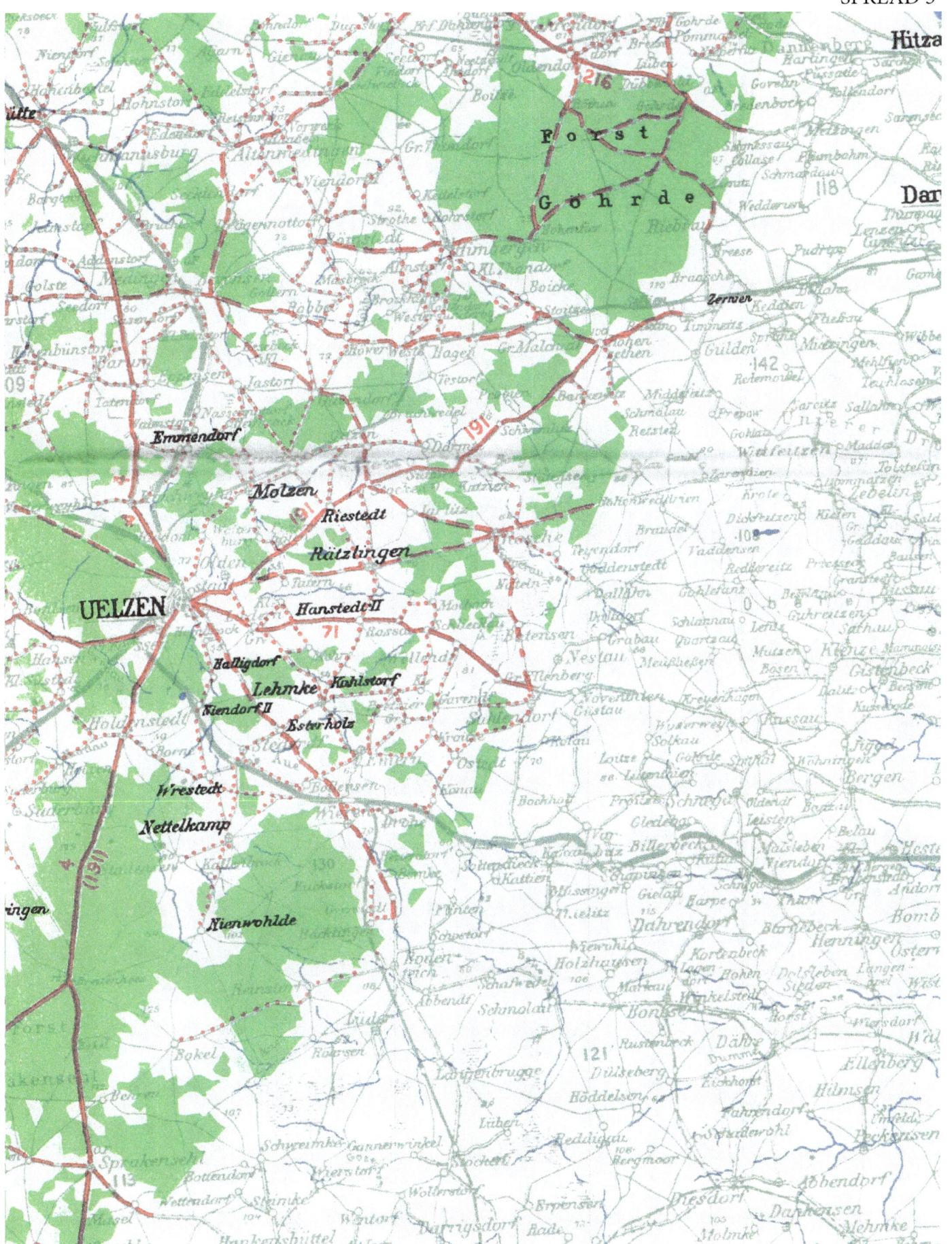

SPREAD 6

SPREAD 6

SPREAD 7

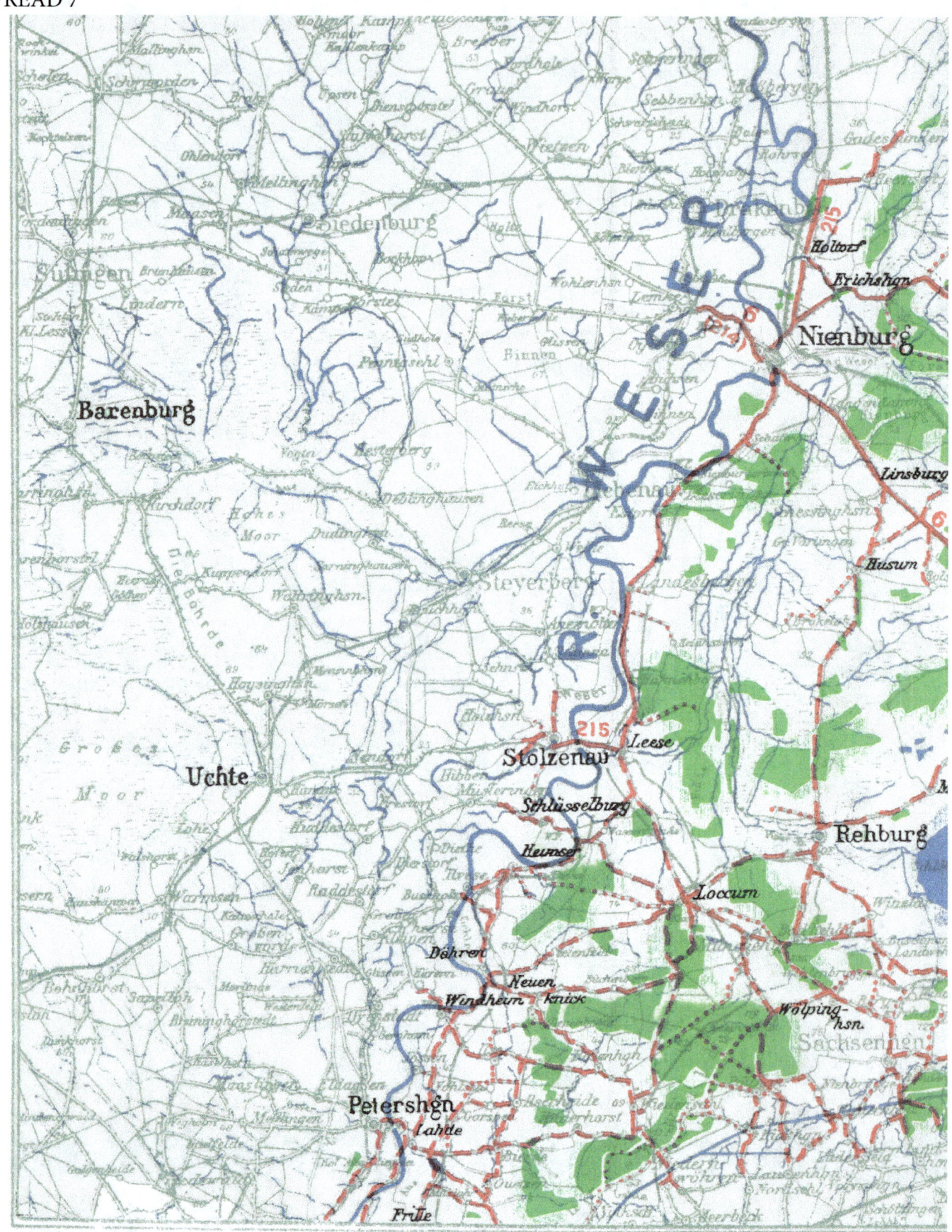

B.C./Misc/151

SPREAD 7

SPREAD 8

SPREAD 8

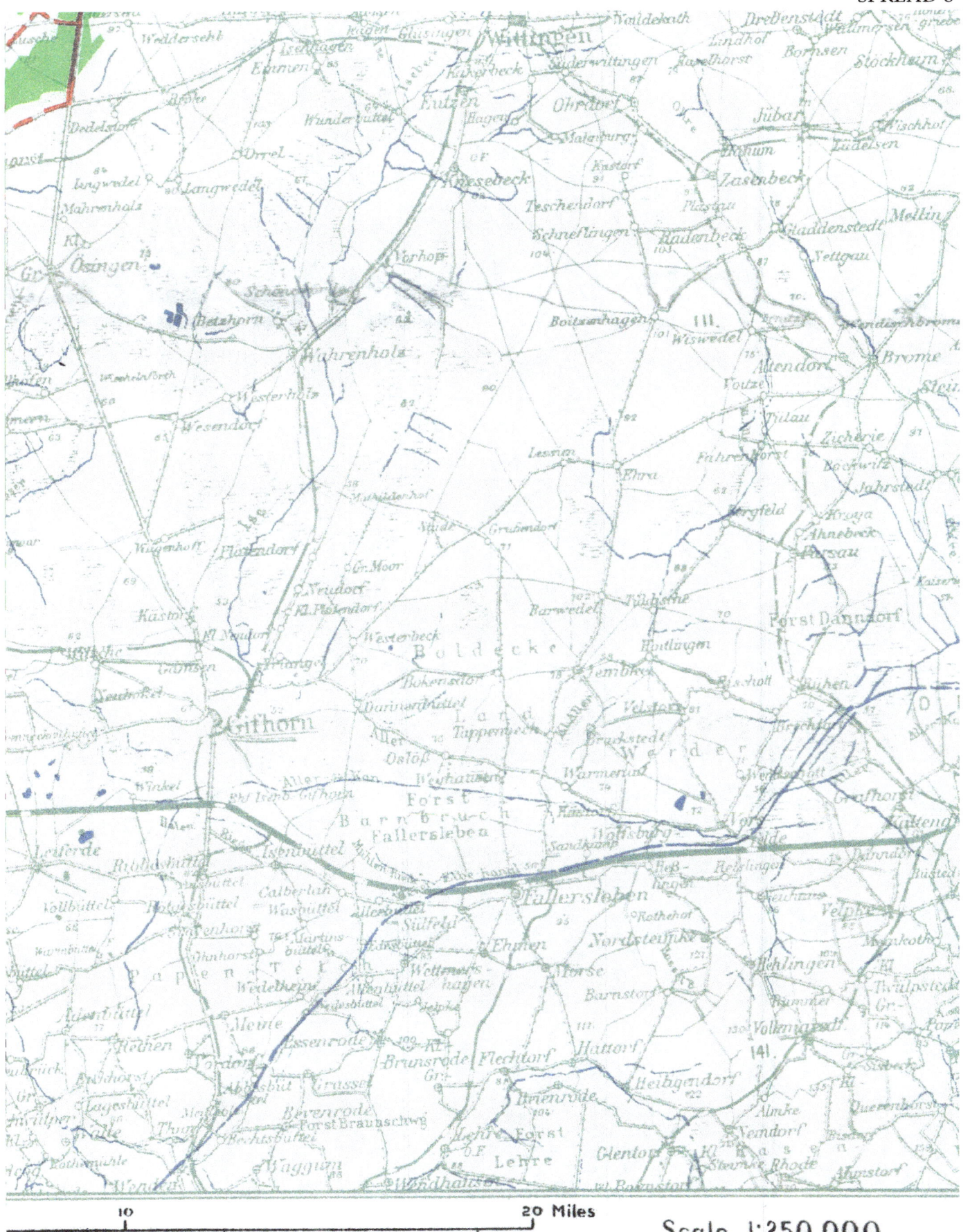

Scale 1:250,000

SPREAD 9

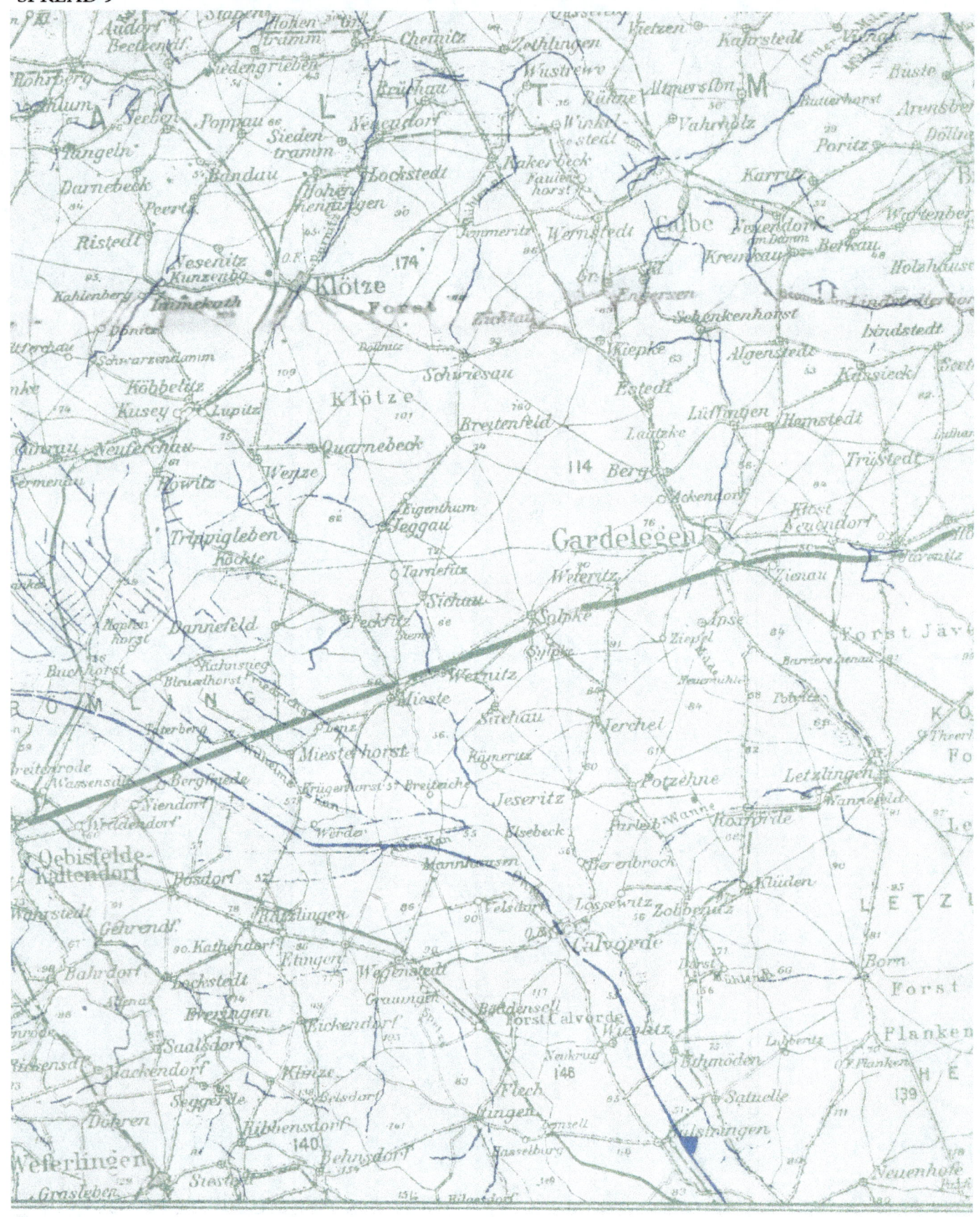

SPREAD 9

,000,000

1 Millimetre = 1 Kilometre

60 70 80 90 100 110 120 130 Miles

100 120 140 160 180 200 Kilometres

Main Corps Axis

Subsidiary Axis

9 Apr Corps HQ Locations

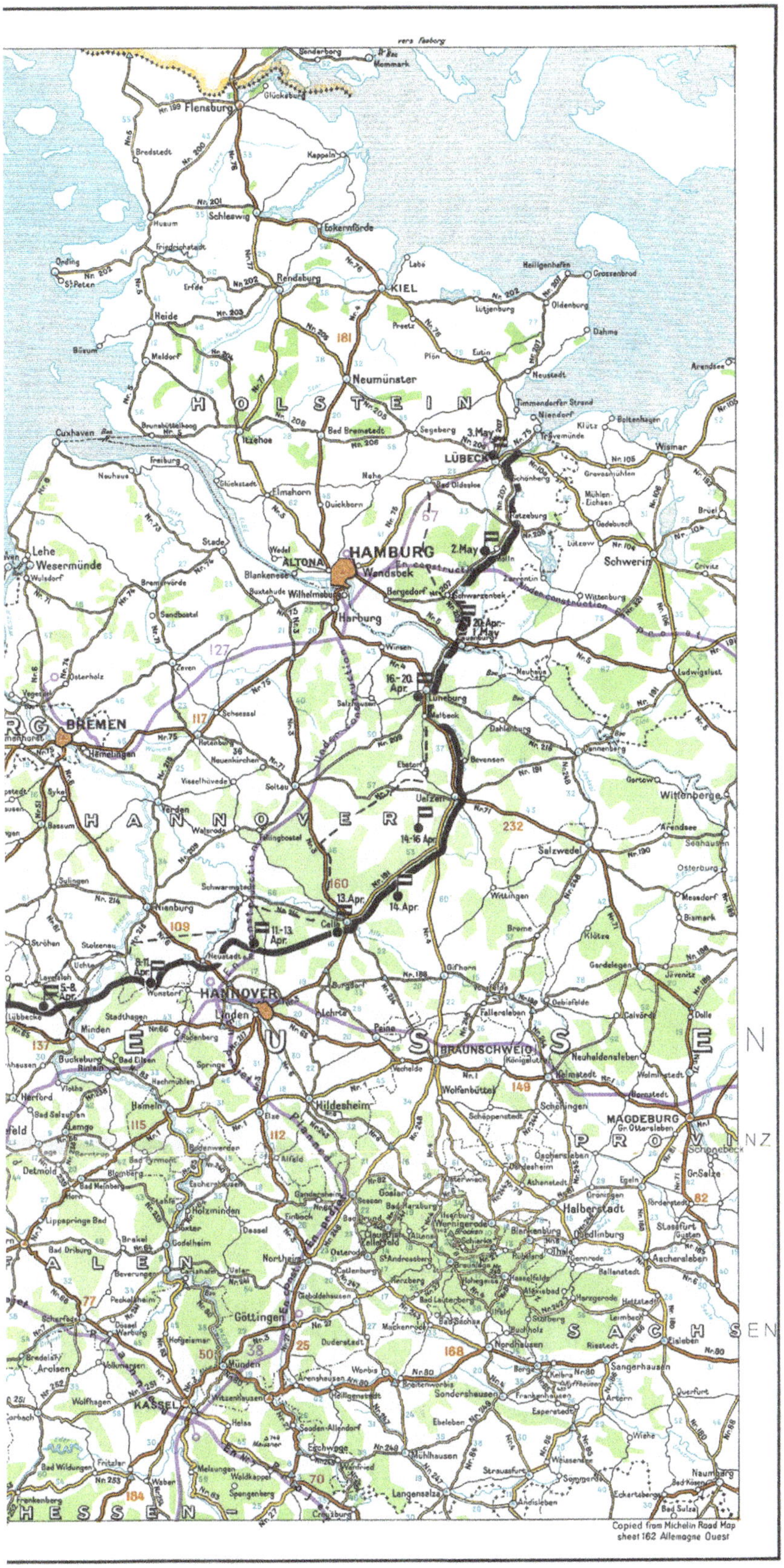

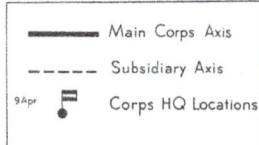

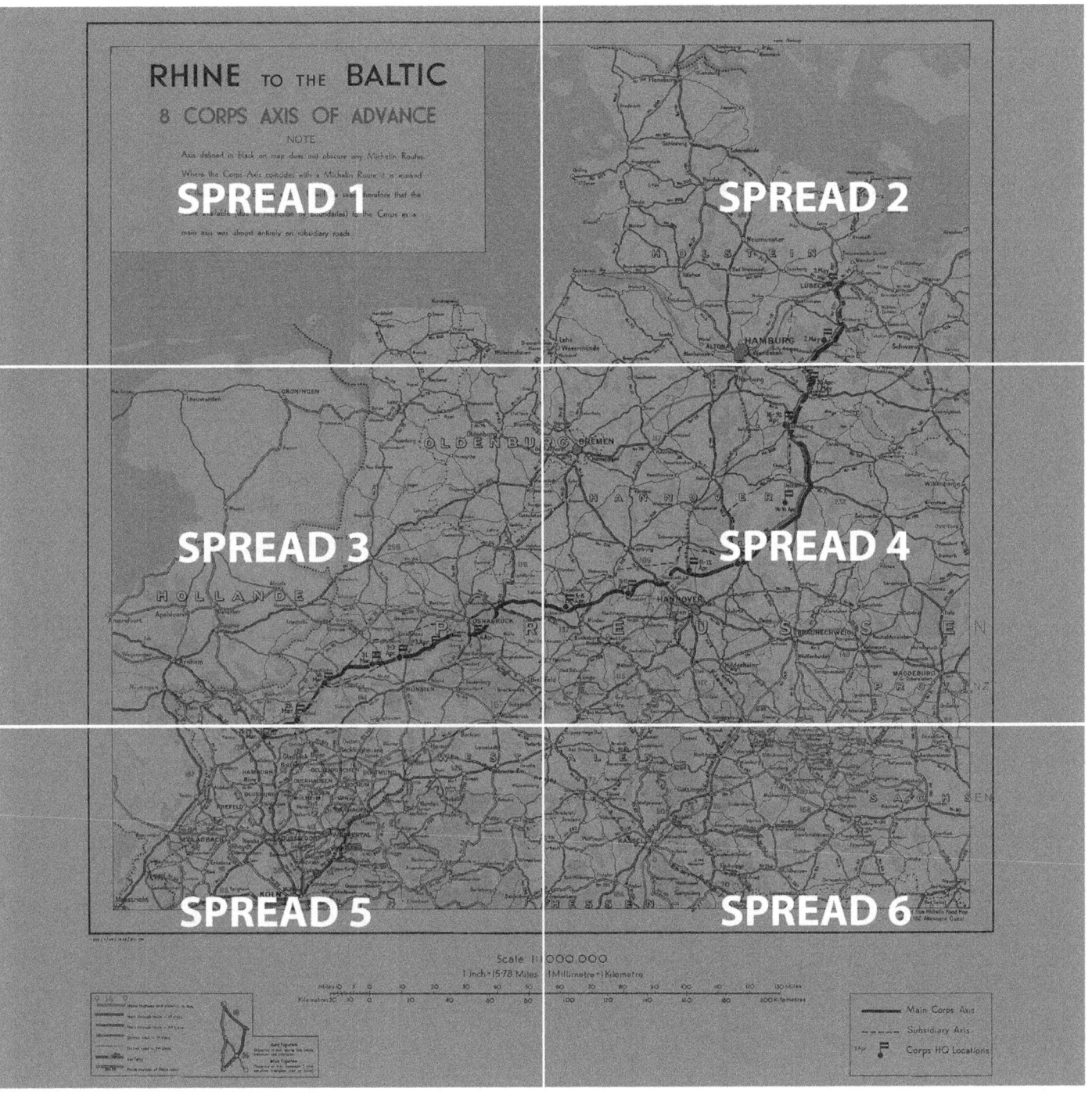

SPREAD 1

O THE BALTIC

XIS OF ADVANCE

NOTE

map does not obscure any Michelin Routes.

oincides with a Michelin Route it is marked

rn edge. It will be seen therefore that the

striction by boundaries) to the Corps as a

rely on subsidiary roads.

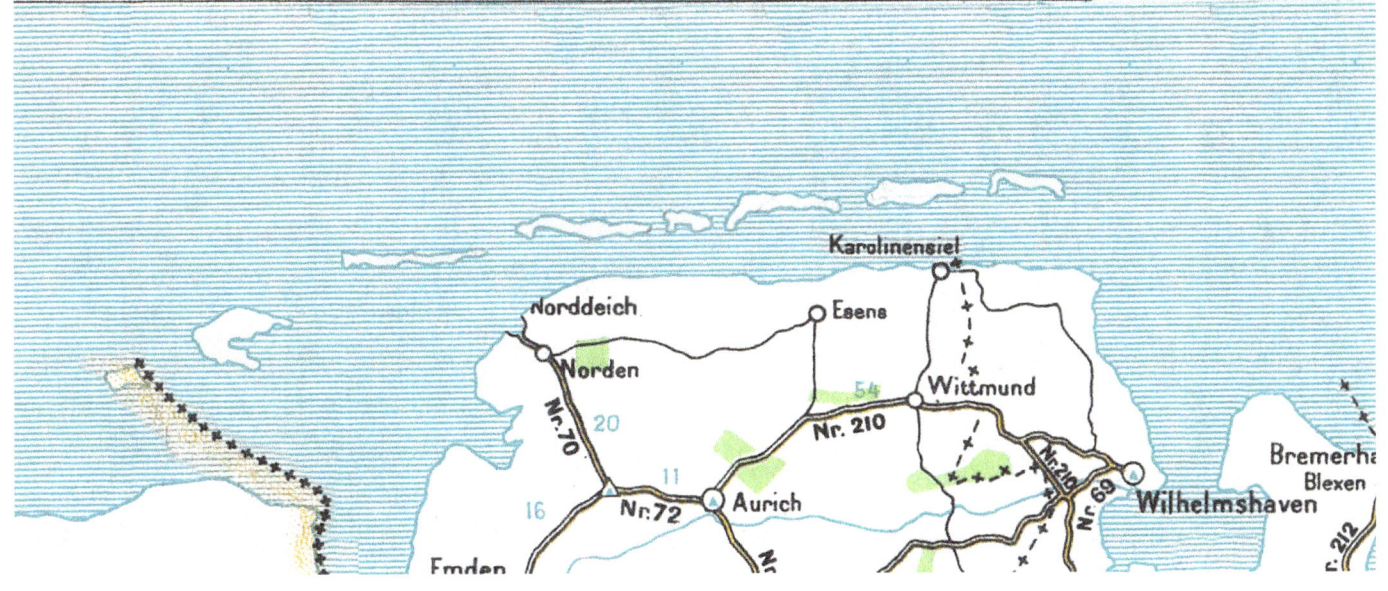

SPREAD 2

SPREAD 2

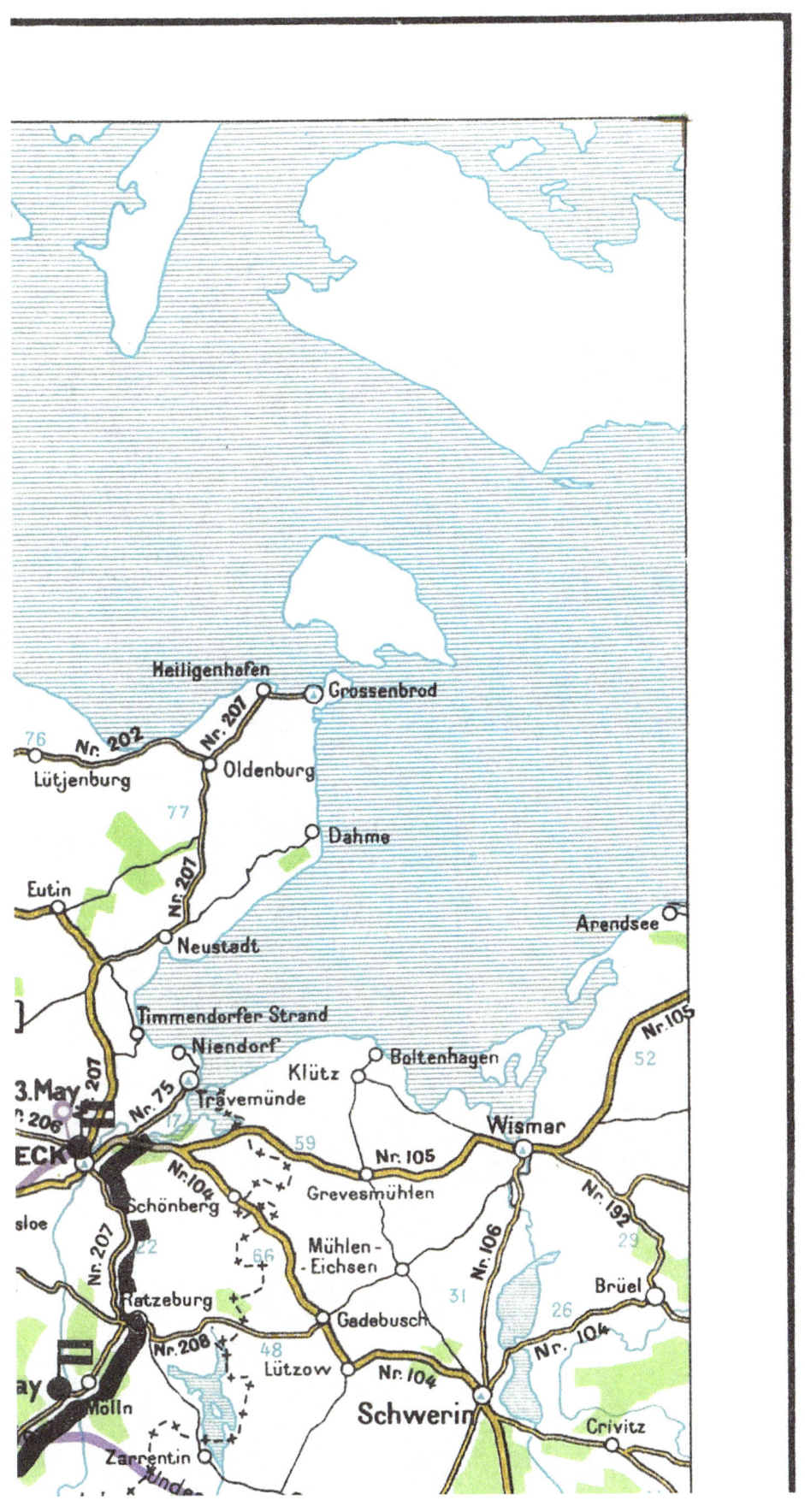

SPREAD 3

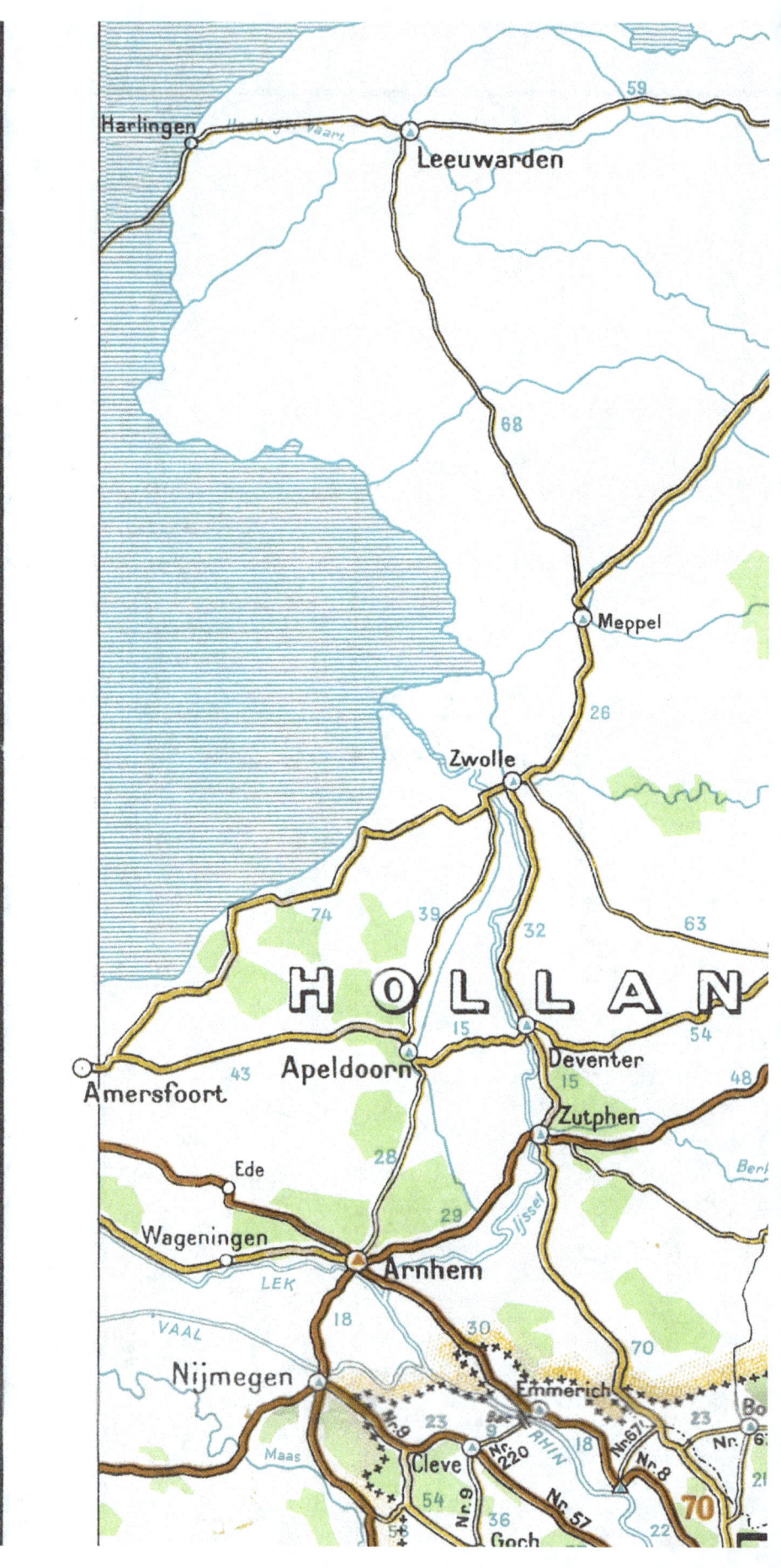

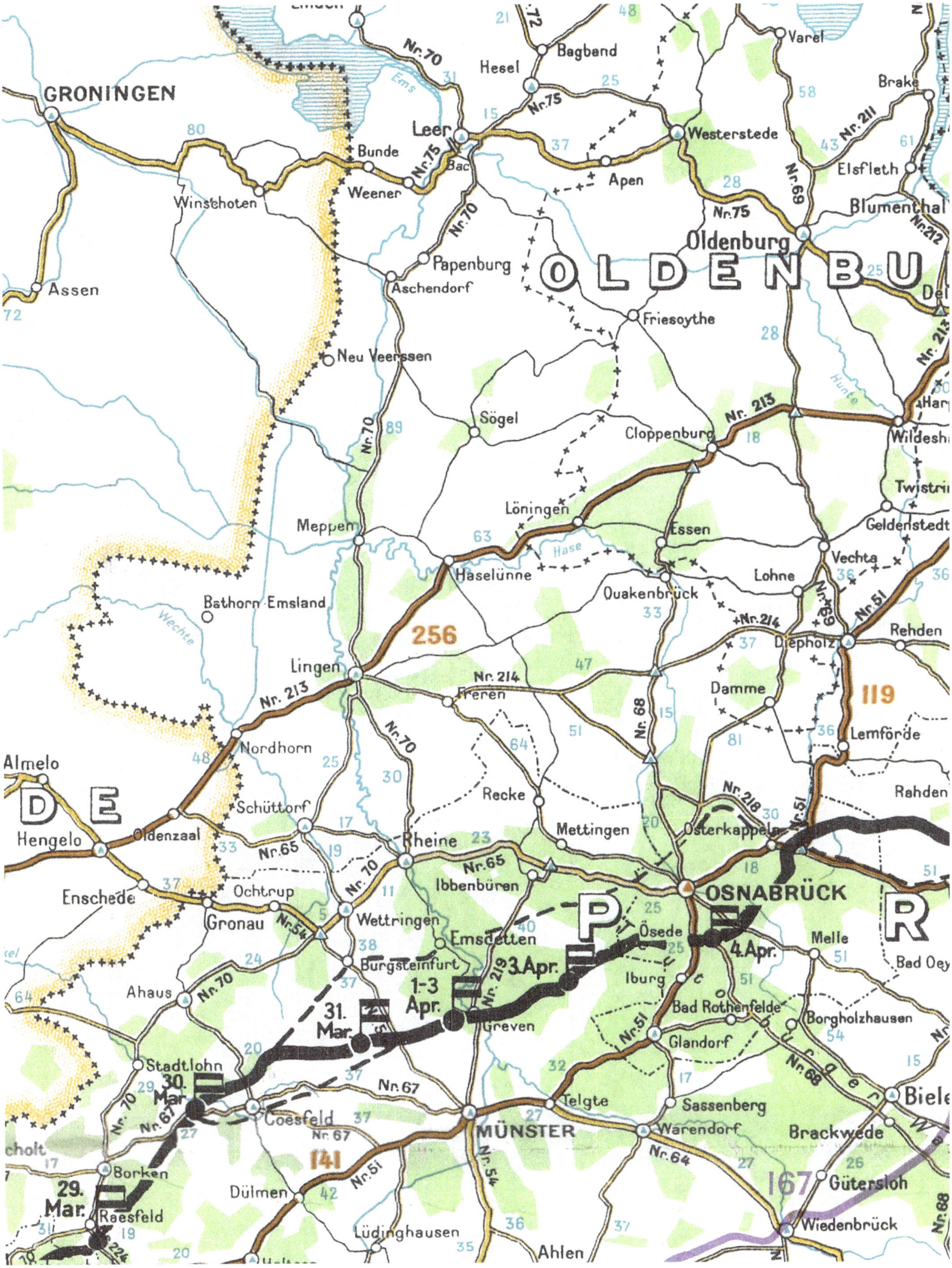
GRONINGEN
Assen
Winschoten
Bunde
Weener
Leer
Hesel
Bagband
Varel
Brake
Westerstede
Apen
Elsfleth
Blumenthal
Oldenburg
OLDENBU
Papenburg
Aschendorf
Friesoythe
Neu Veerssen
Sögel
Cloppenburg
Wildesh
Twistri
Löningen
Essen
Geldenstedt
Meppen
Haselünne
Vechta
Quakenbrück
Lohne
Bathorn Emsland
256
Diepholz
Rehden
Lingen
Freren
Damme
119
Lemförde
Nordhorn
Almelo
Recke
Rahden
D E
Hengelo
Oldenzaal
Schüttorf
Rheine
Mettingen
Osterkappeln
Enschede
Ochtrup
Ibbenbüren
OSNABRÜCK
Gronau
Wettringen
Emsdetten
P
Ösede
R
Melle
4.Apr.
Bad Oey
Burgsteinfurt
3.Apr.
Iburg
Ahaus
1-3 Apr.
31. Mar.
Greven
Bad Rothenfelde
Borgholzhausen
Glandorf
Stadtlohn
30. Mar.
Coesfeld
Telgte
Sassenberg
Biele
MÜNSTER
Warendorf
Brackwede
Borken
141
Gütersloh
167
29. Mar.
Raesfeld
Dülmen
Wiedenbrück
Lüdinghausen
Ahlen
Nr. 70
Nr. 75
Nr. 213
Nr. 214
Nr. 69
Nr. 68
Nr. 65
Nr. 67
Nr. 51
Nr. 54
Nr. 64
Nr. 218
Nr. 211
Nr. 212
Ems
Hase
Hunte
Wechte

SPREAD 4

SPREAD 4

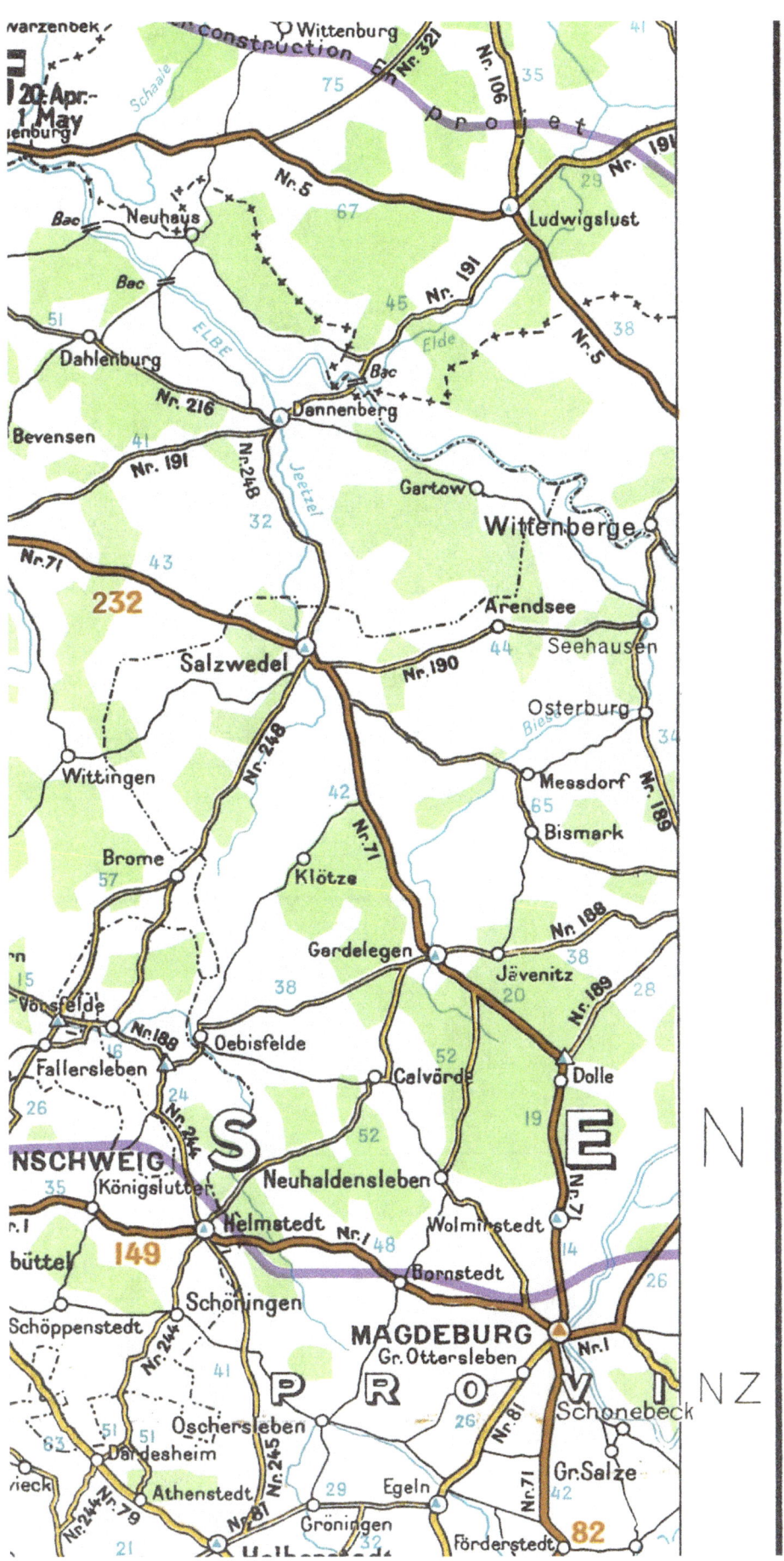

SPREAD 5

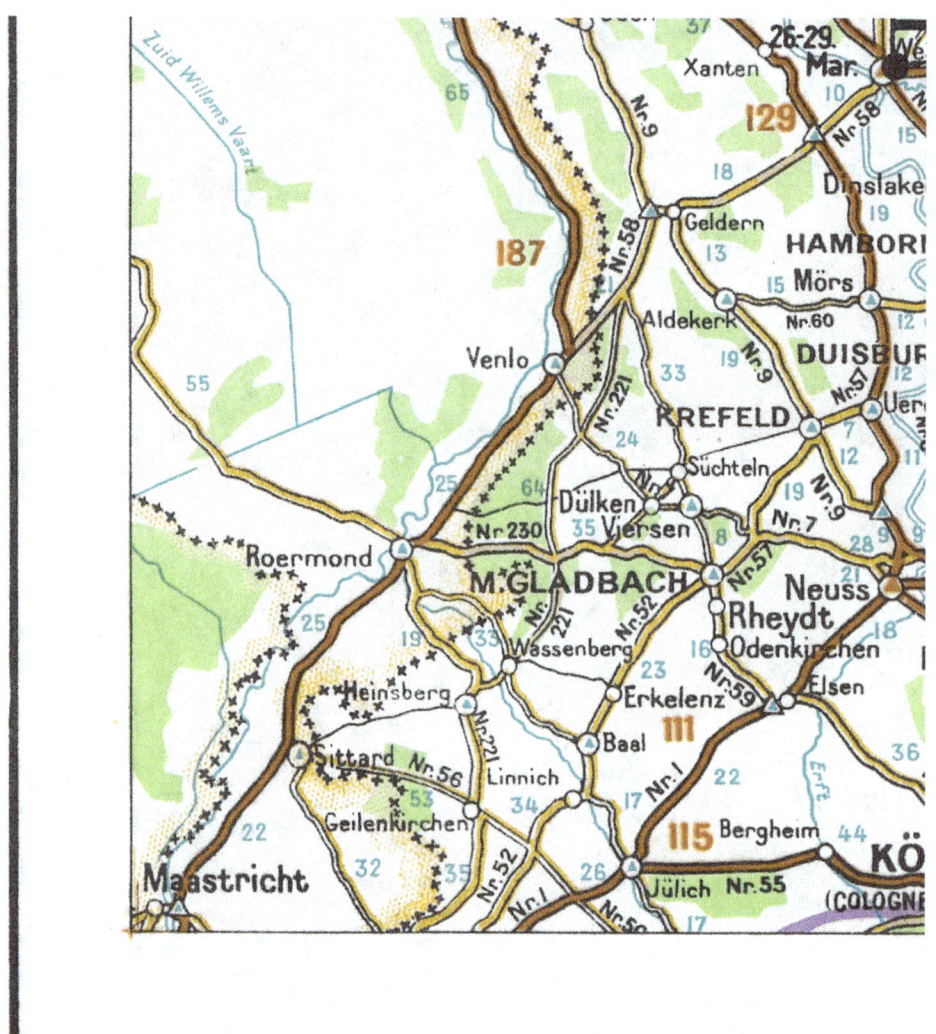

1.500 / 1 / 46 / 14 R.E. / BC. 154

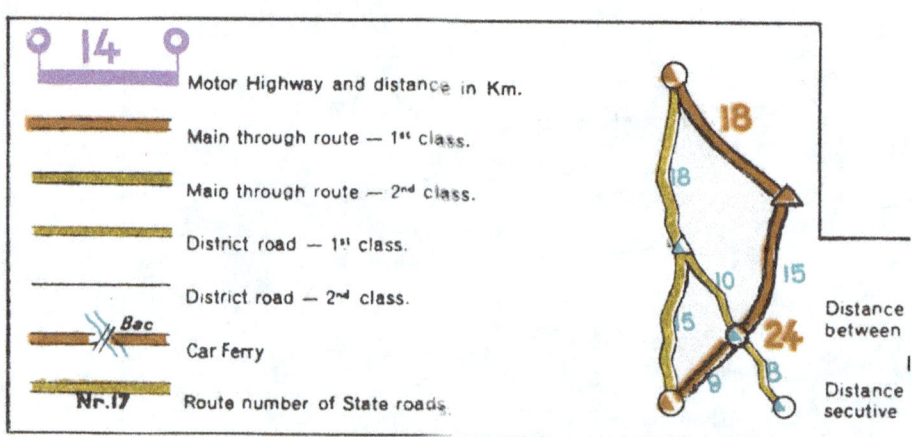

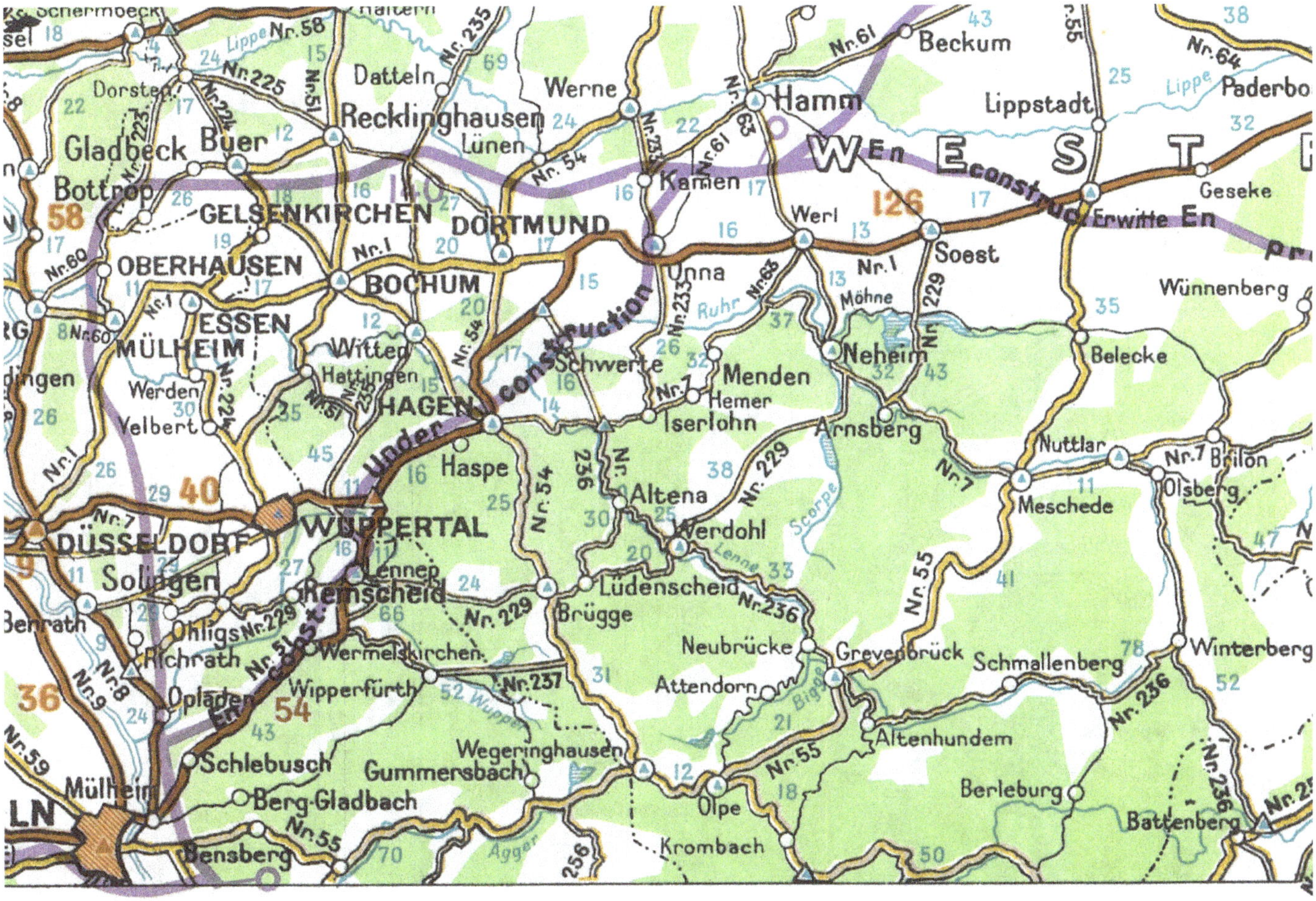

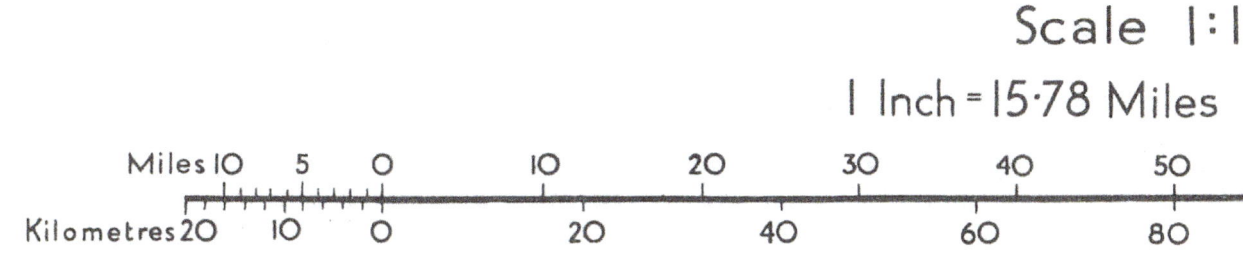

Scale 1:1

1 Inch = 15·78 Miles

Miles 10 5 0 10 20 30 40 50

Kilometres 20 10 0 20 40 60 80

Red Figures
in Km. along red roads,
red triangles.

Blue Figures
in Km. between 2 con-
triangles (red or blue).

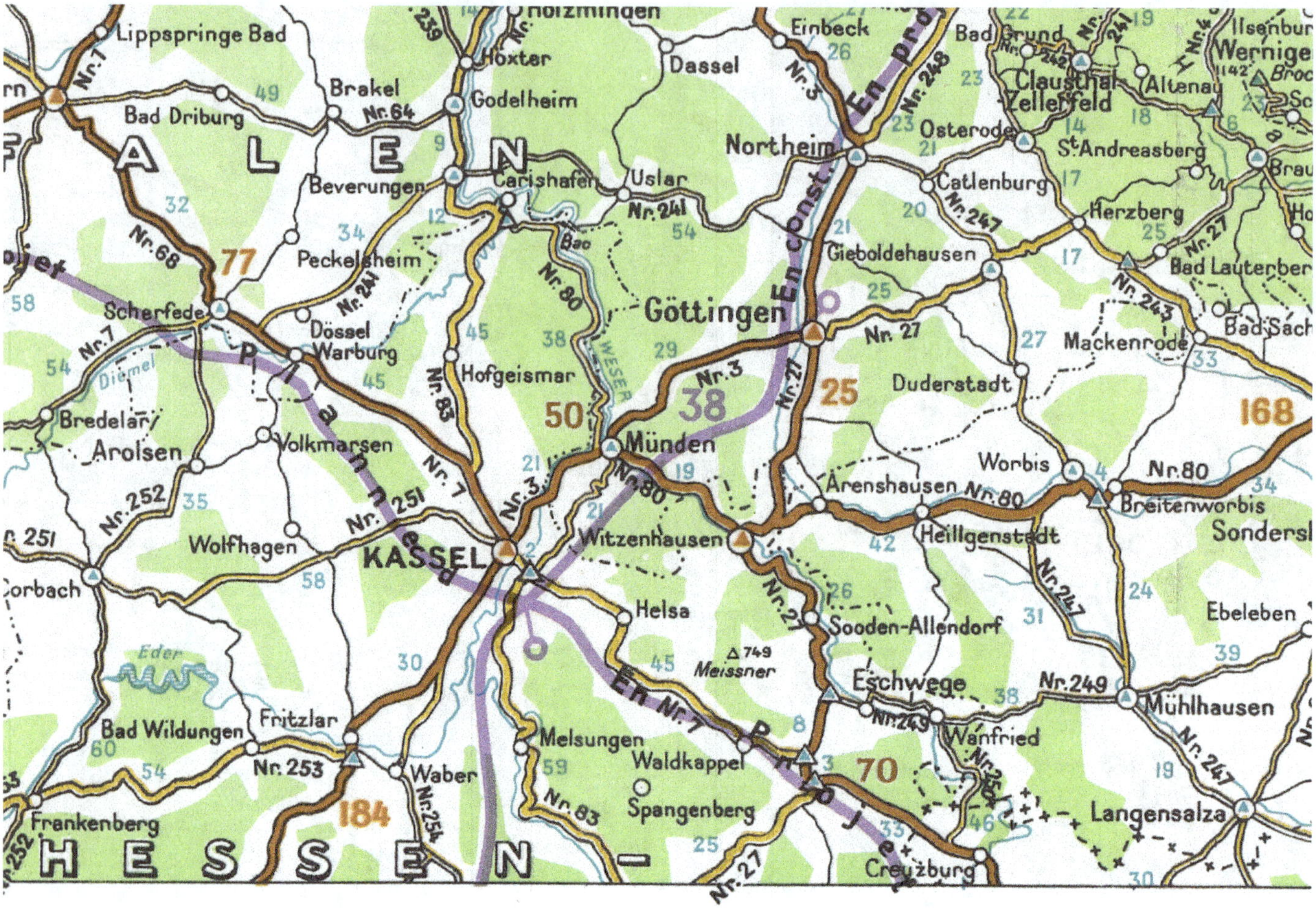

SPREAD 6

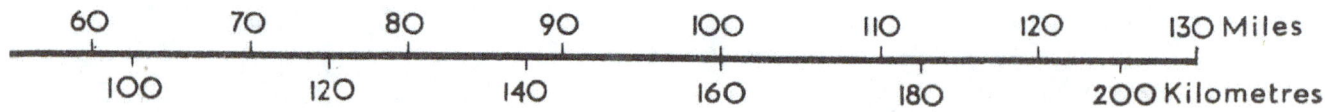

,000,000

1 Millimetre = 1 Kilometre

60　　70　　80　　90　　100　　110　　120　　130 Miles

100　　120　　140　　160　　180　　200 Kilometres

SPREAD 6

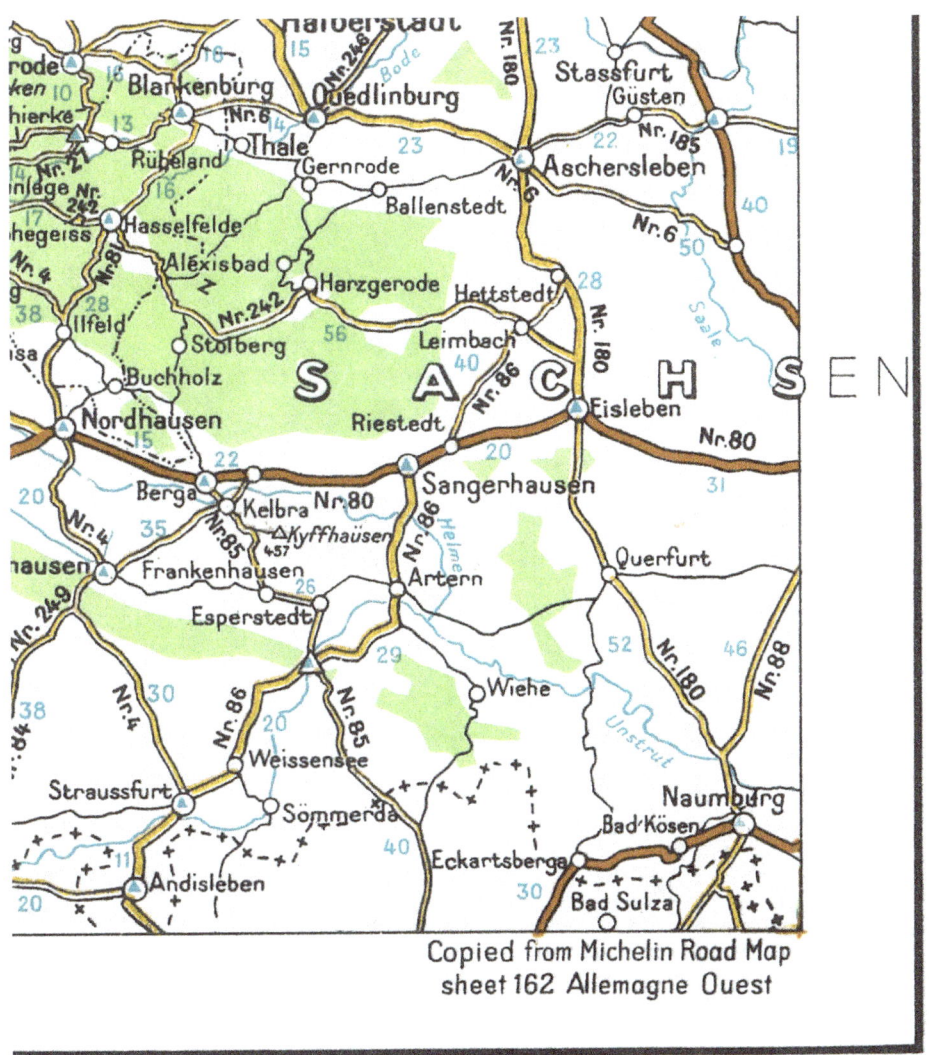

Copied from Michelin Road Map sheet 162 Allemagne Ouest

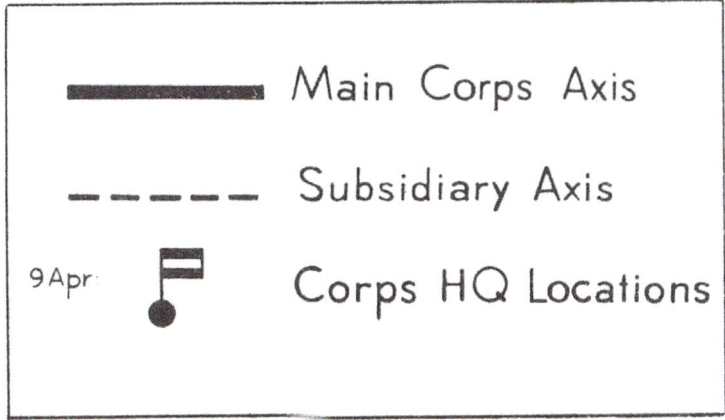

ELBE TO BALTIC

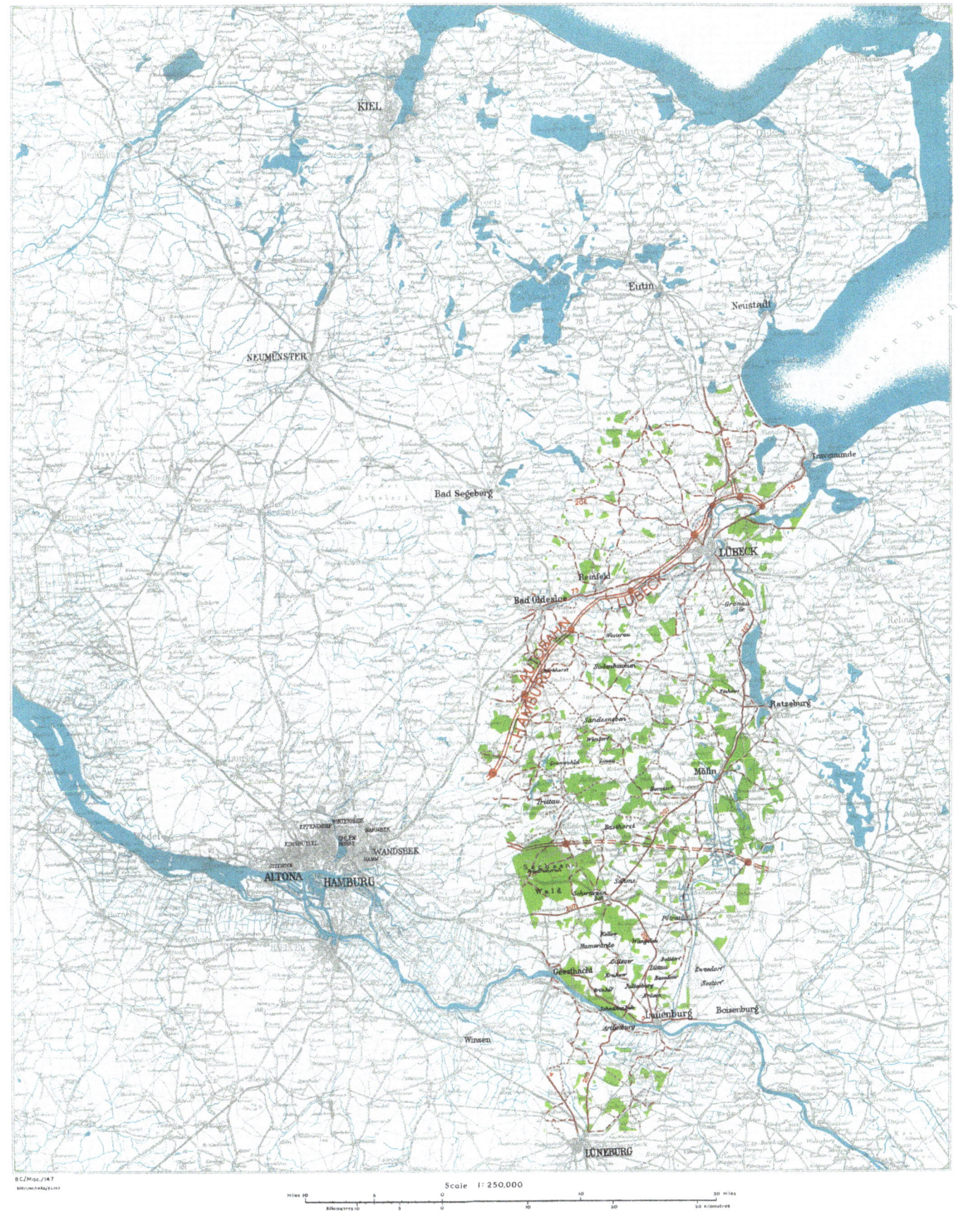

Scale 1:250,000

ELBE TO BALTIC

SPREAD 1 | SPREAD 2
SPREAD 3 | SPREAD 4
SPREAD 5 | SPREAD 6

SPREAD 1

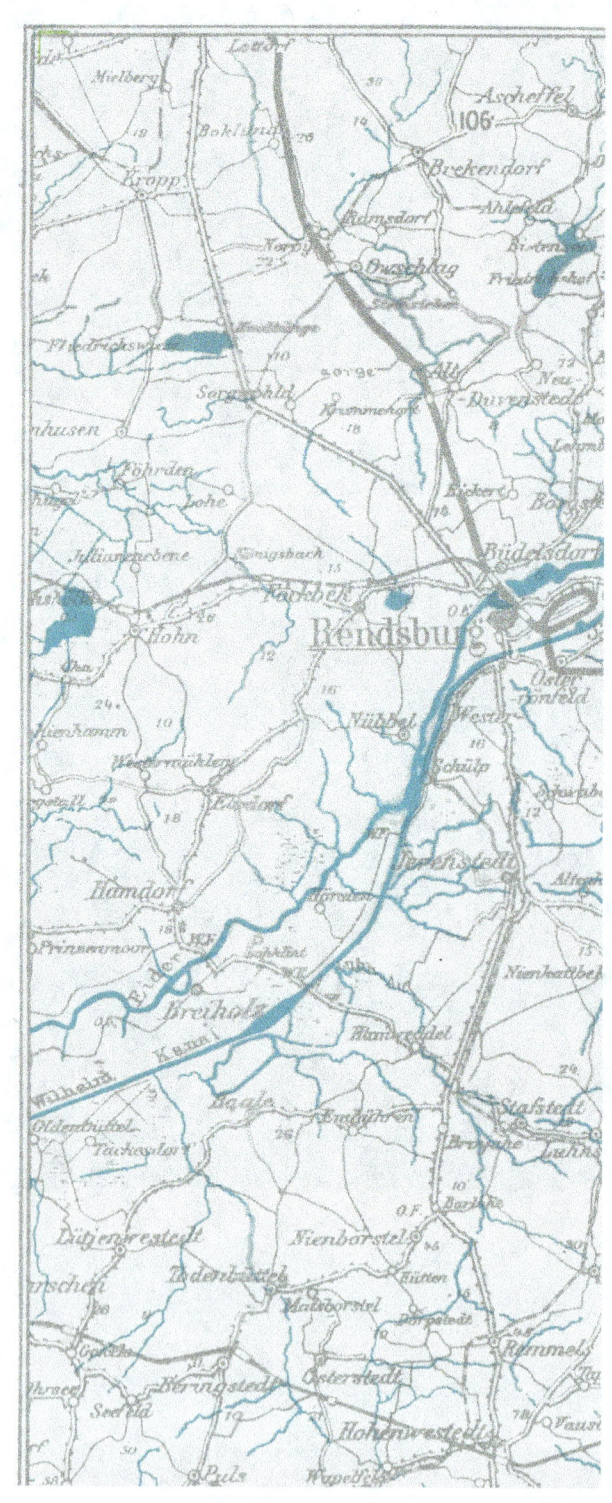

ELBE TO

SPREAD 2

BALTIC

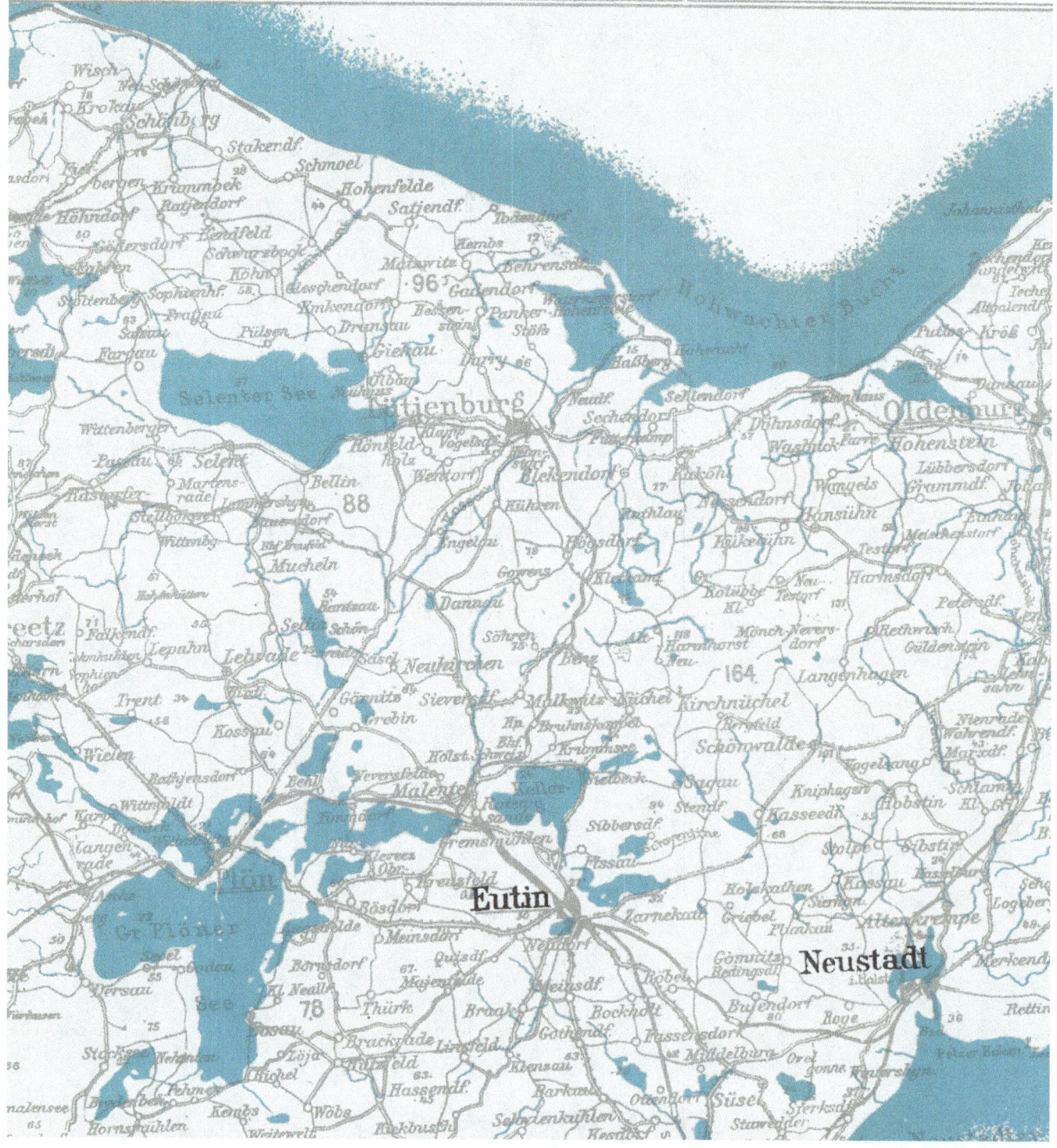

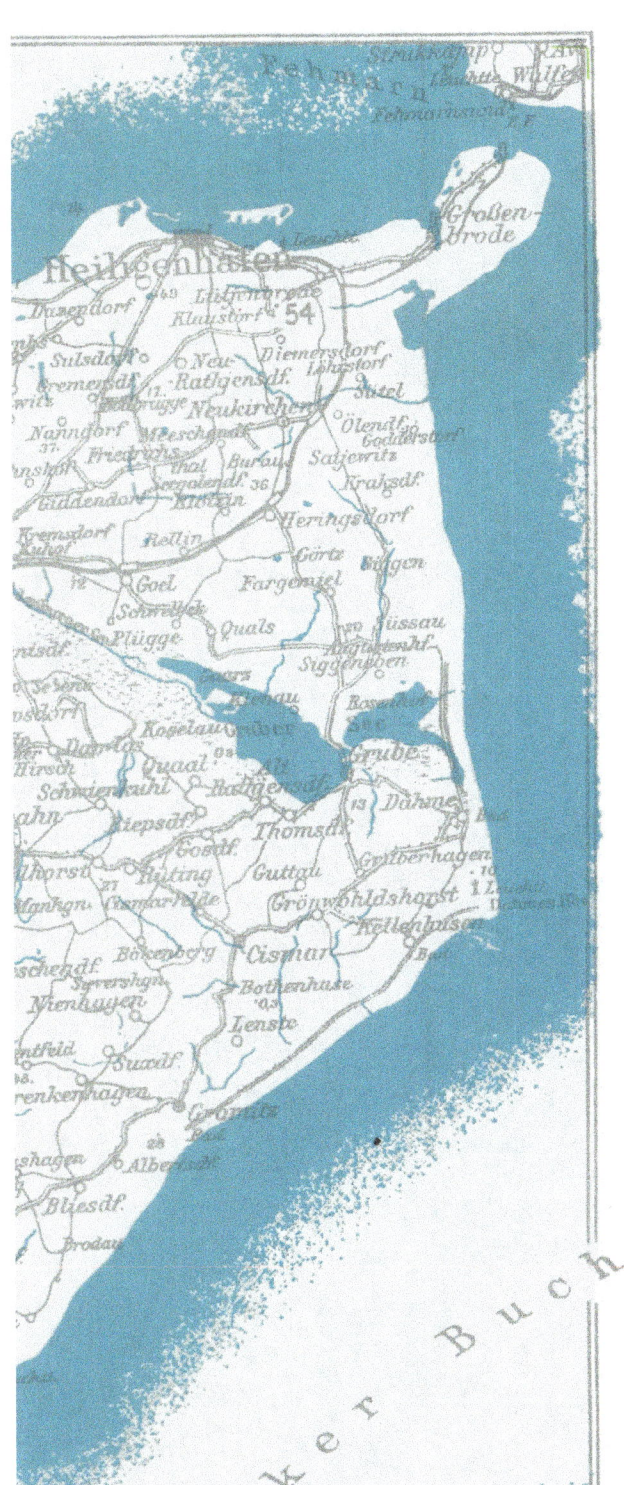

SPREAD 3

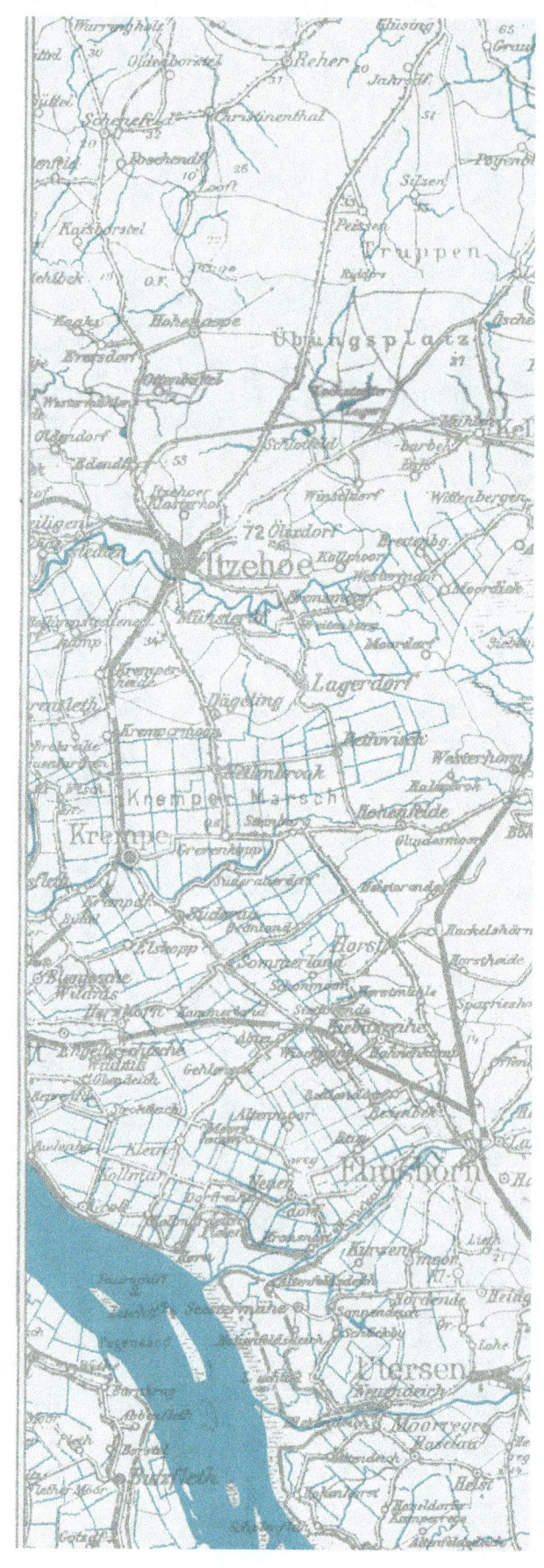

SPREAD 3

SPREAD 4

SPREAD 4

SPREAD 5

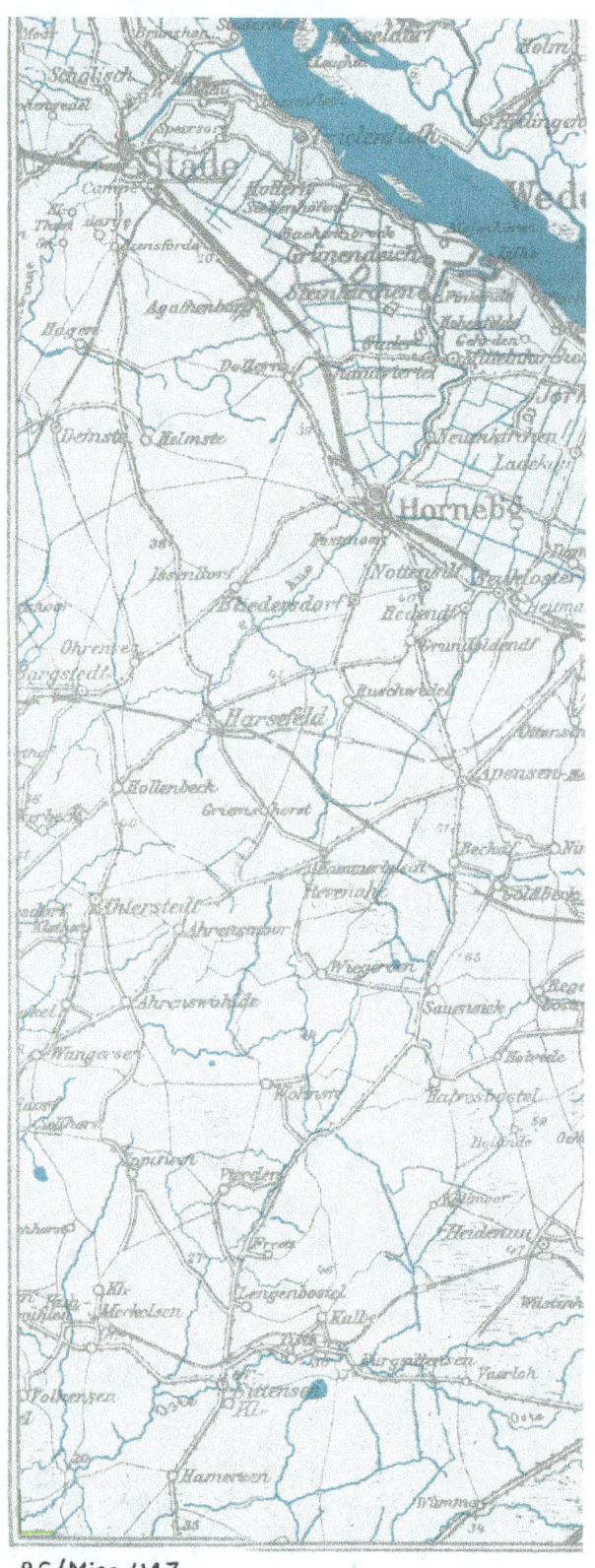

8 C./Misc./147
500/1/46/14 RE/8.C.147

WINTERHUDE
EPPENDORF
BARMBEK
UHLEN HORST
EIMSBÜTTEL
WANDSBEK
HAMM
OTTENSEN
ALTONA
HAMBURG
WILHELMSBURG
HARBURG
Buxtehude
Buchholz
Scale 1:
Miles 10 5 0
Kilometres 10 5 0

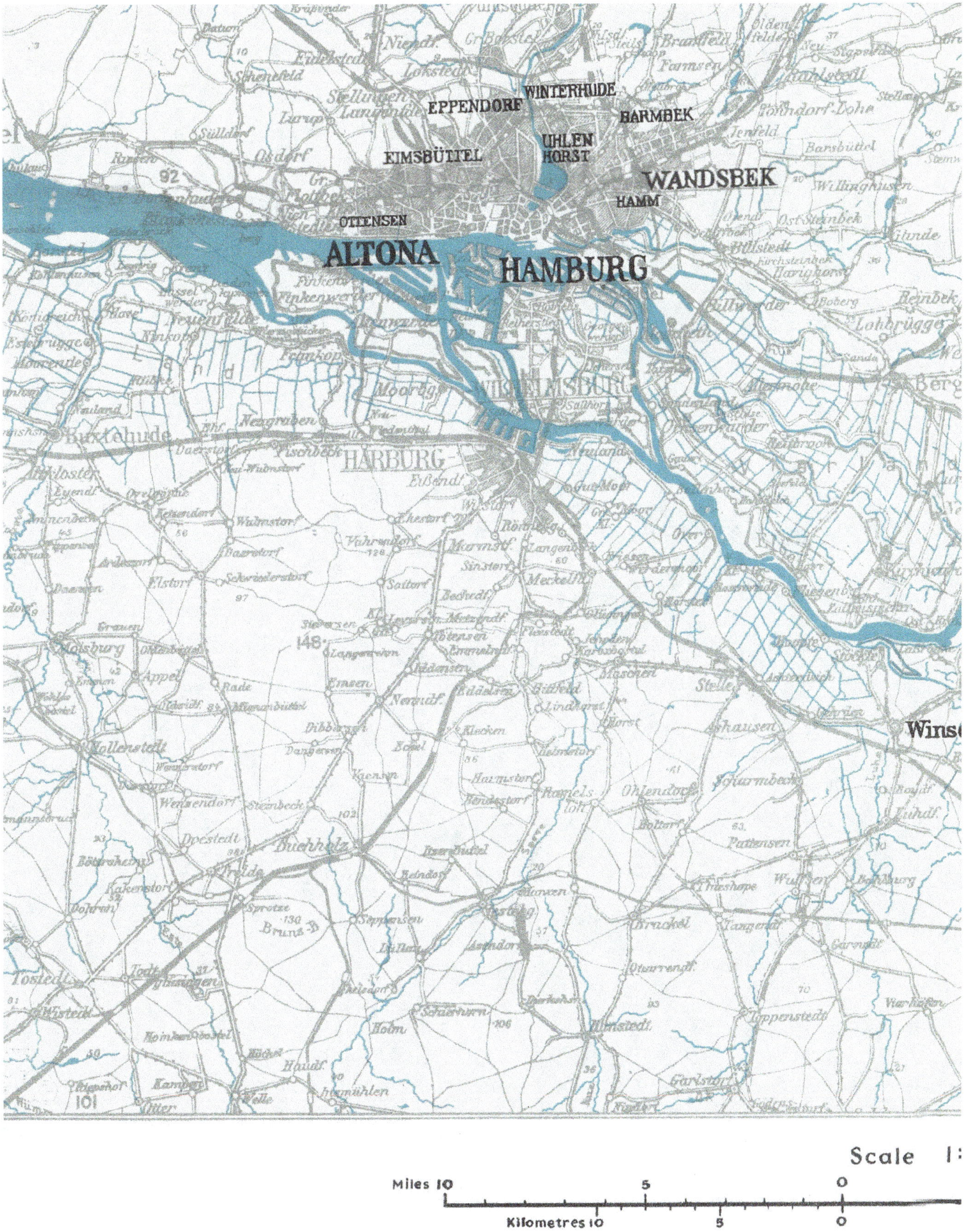

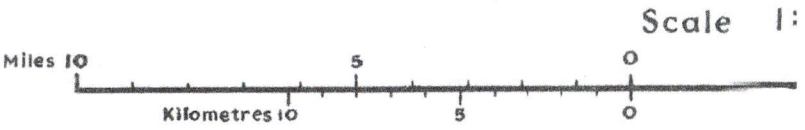

SPREAD 6

Trittau
Basthorst
Sachsen-
Friedrichsruh
Wald
Sahms
Schwarzenbek
Pötrau
Kollow
Wangelau
Hamwarde
Gülzow
Dalldorf
Lütau
Geesthacht
Krukow
Basedow
Zweedorf
Nostorf
Juliusburg
Grünhof
Krüzen
Schnakenbek
Lauenburg
Boizenburg
Artlenburg
Elbe
Trave Canal
LÜNEBURG
Scharnebeck
Bleckede
207
209
: 250,000
10
20 Miles
10
20
30 Kilometres

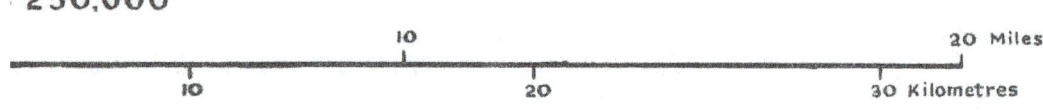

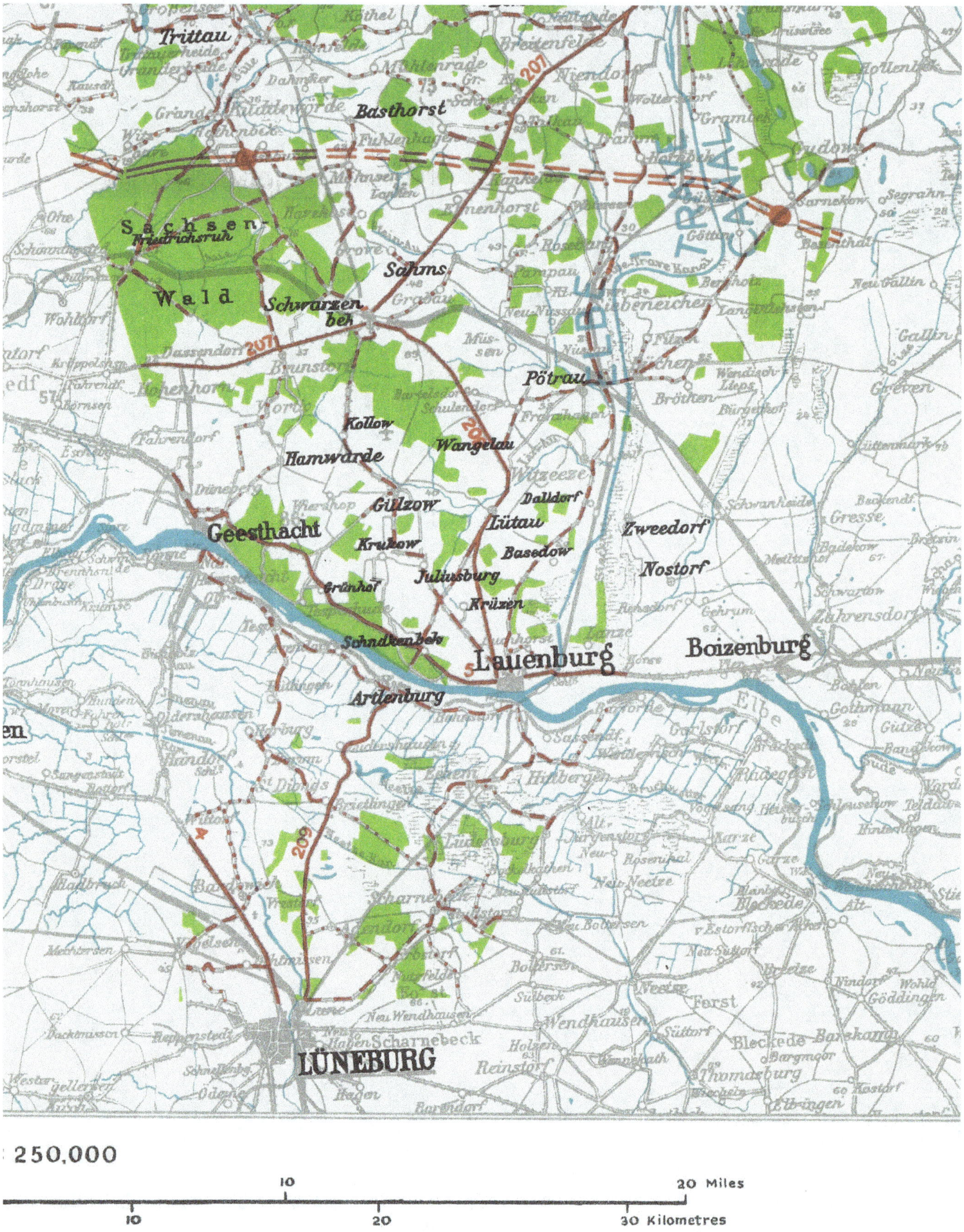

SPREAD 6

RHINE TO

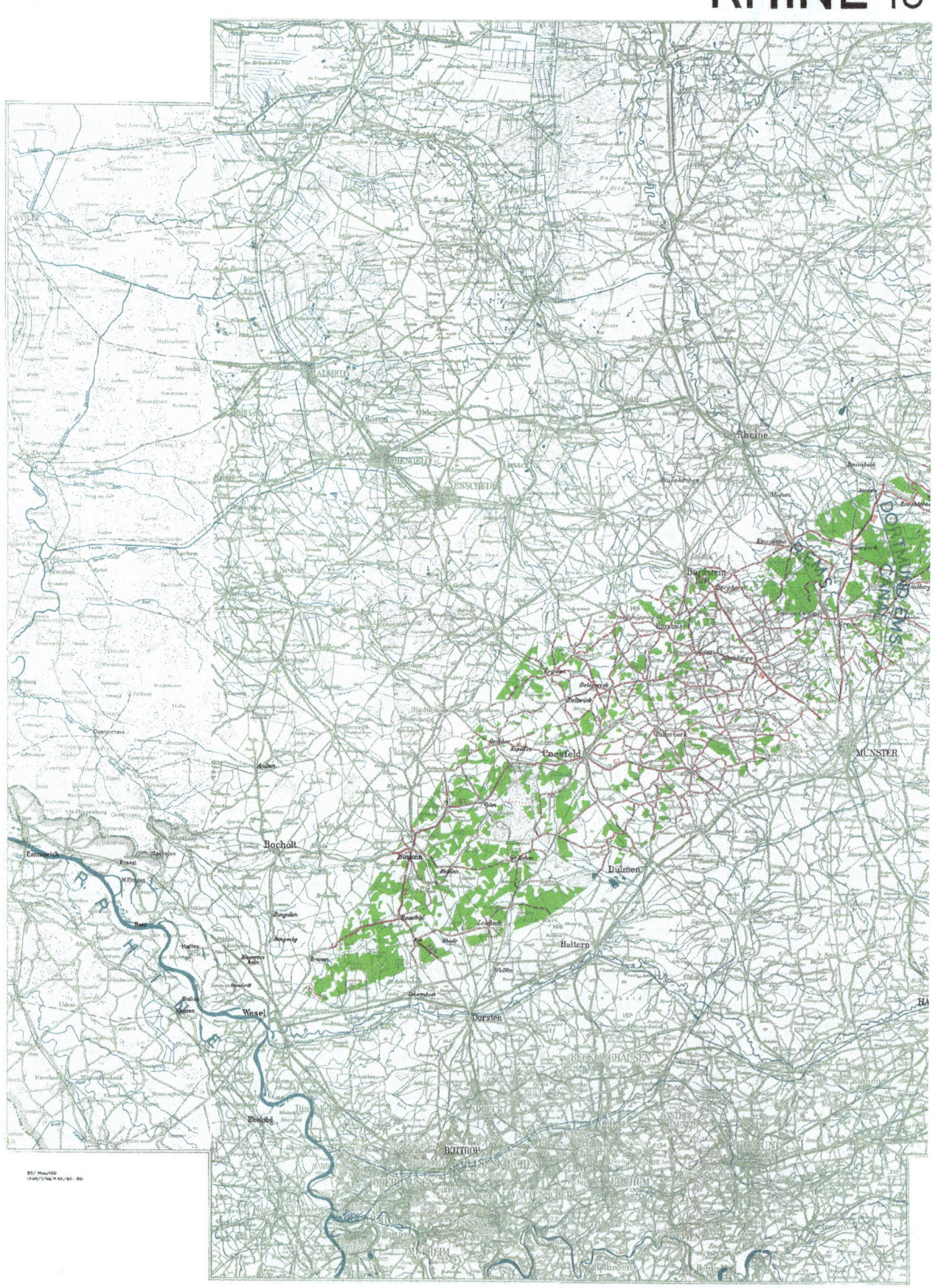

WESER

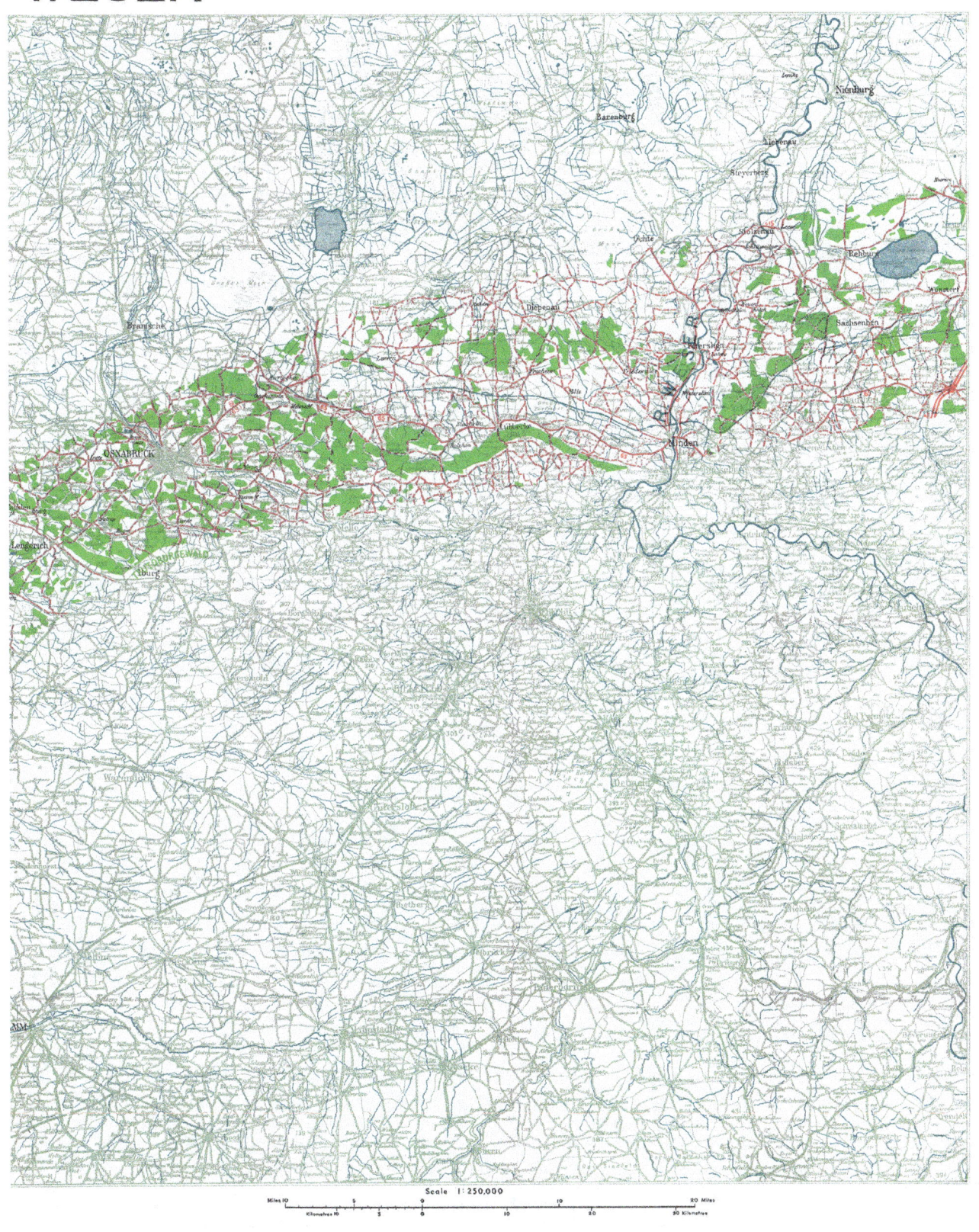

RHINE TO WESER

SPREAD 1	SPREAD 2	SPREAD 3
SPREAD 4	SPREAD 5	SPREAD 6
SPREAD 7	SPREAD 8	SPREAD 9

SPREAD 1

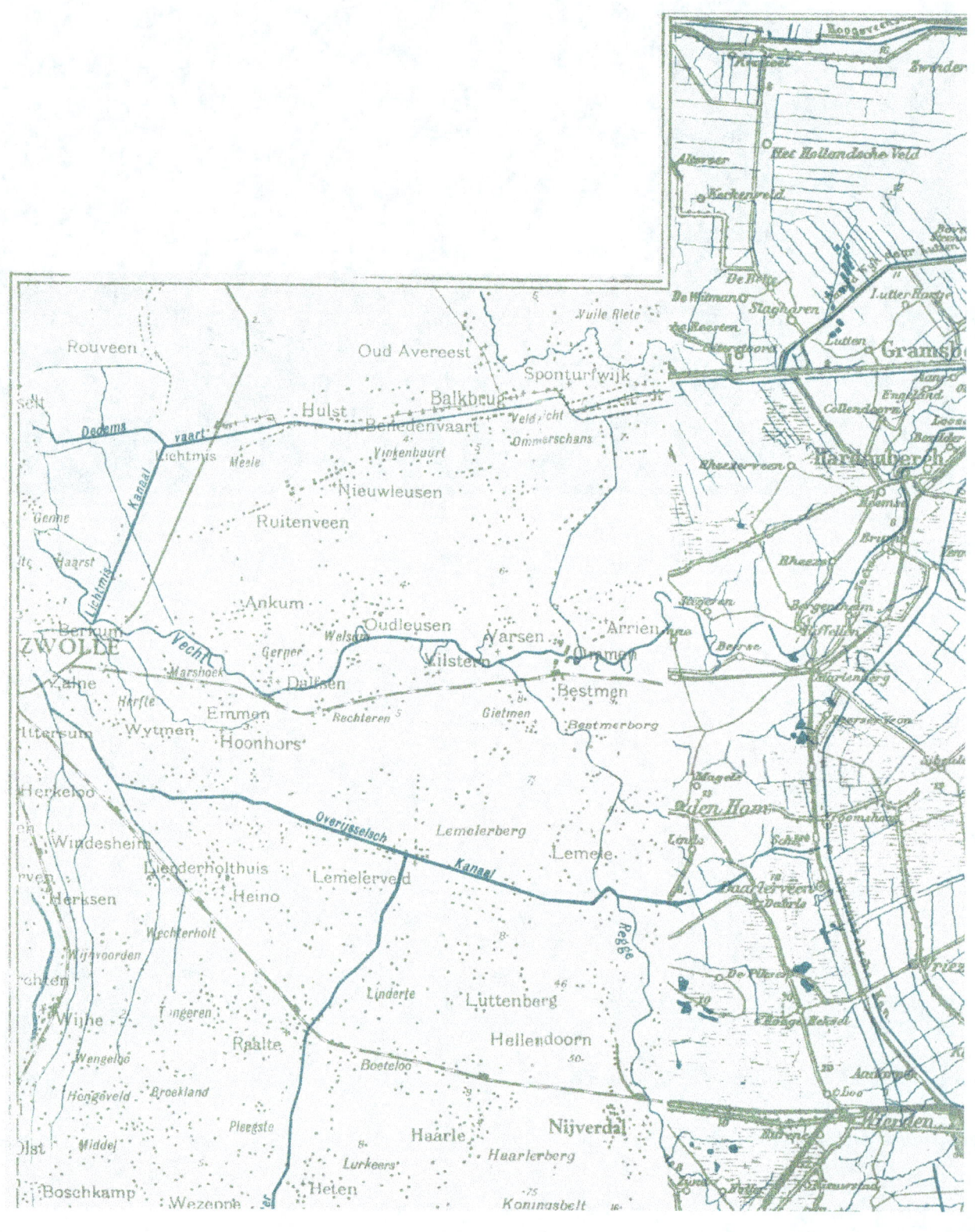

SPREAD 1

SPREAD 2

RHINE TO

WESER

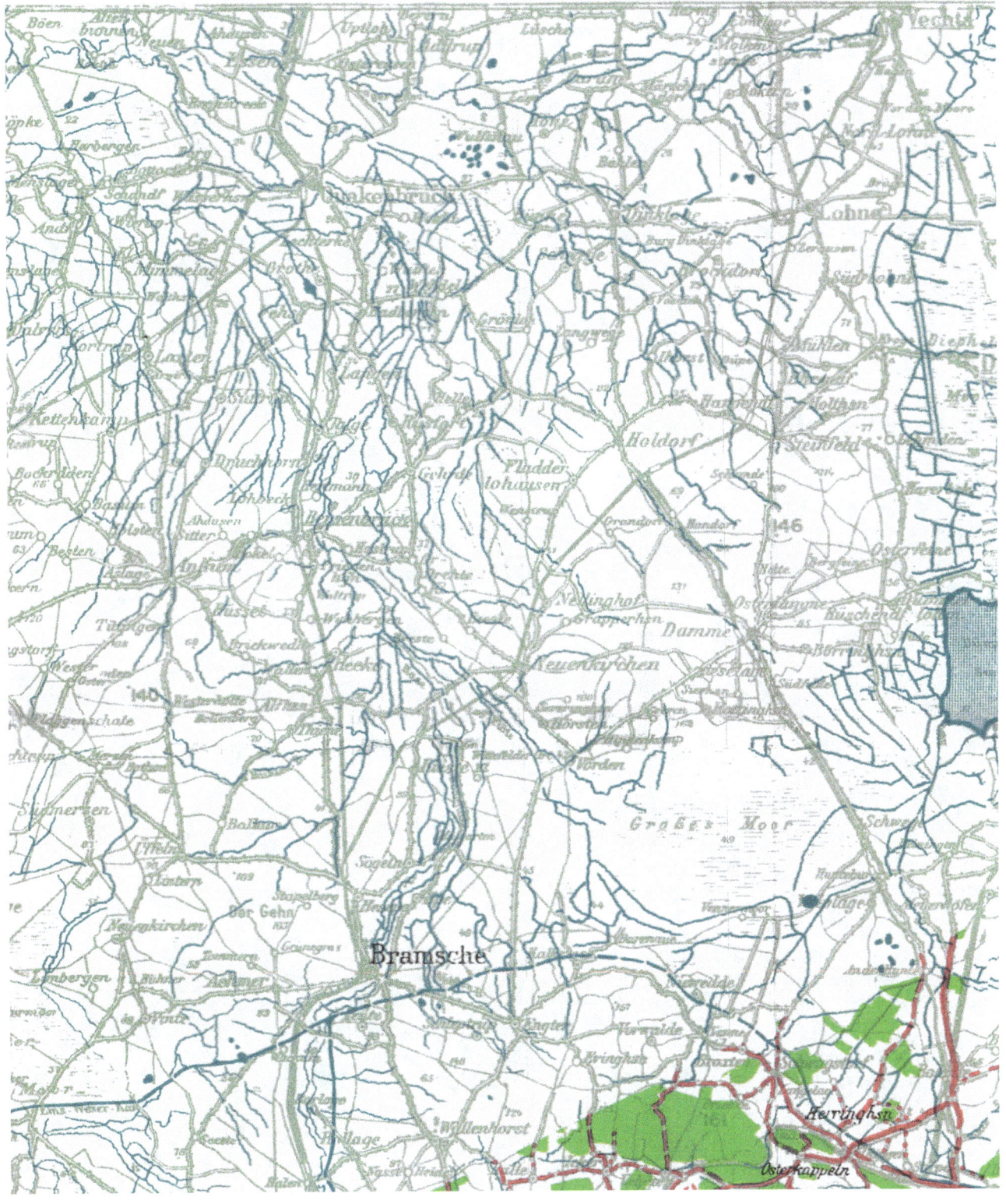

SPREAD 3

SPREAD 3

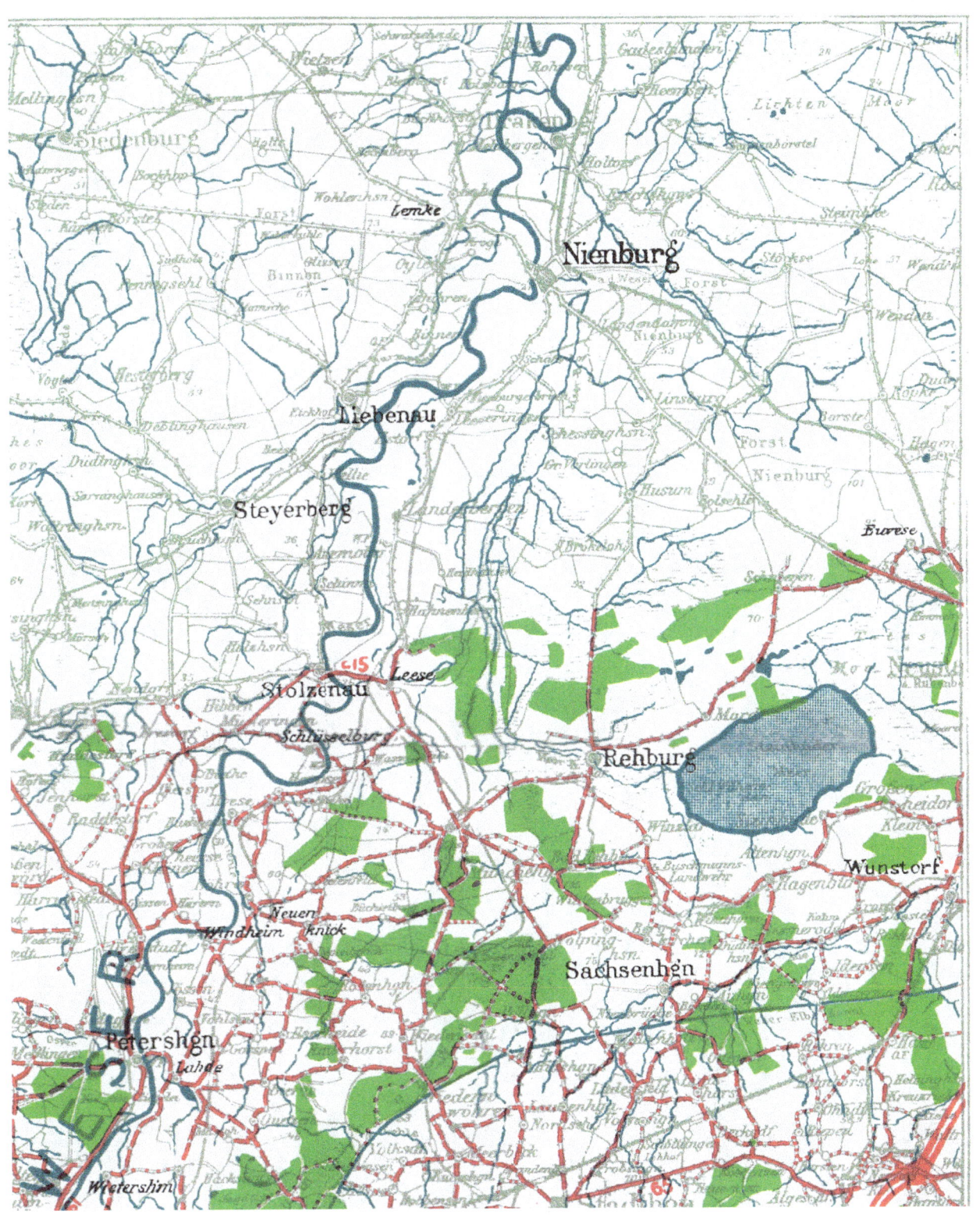

SPREAD 4

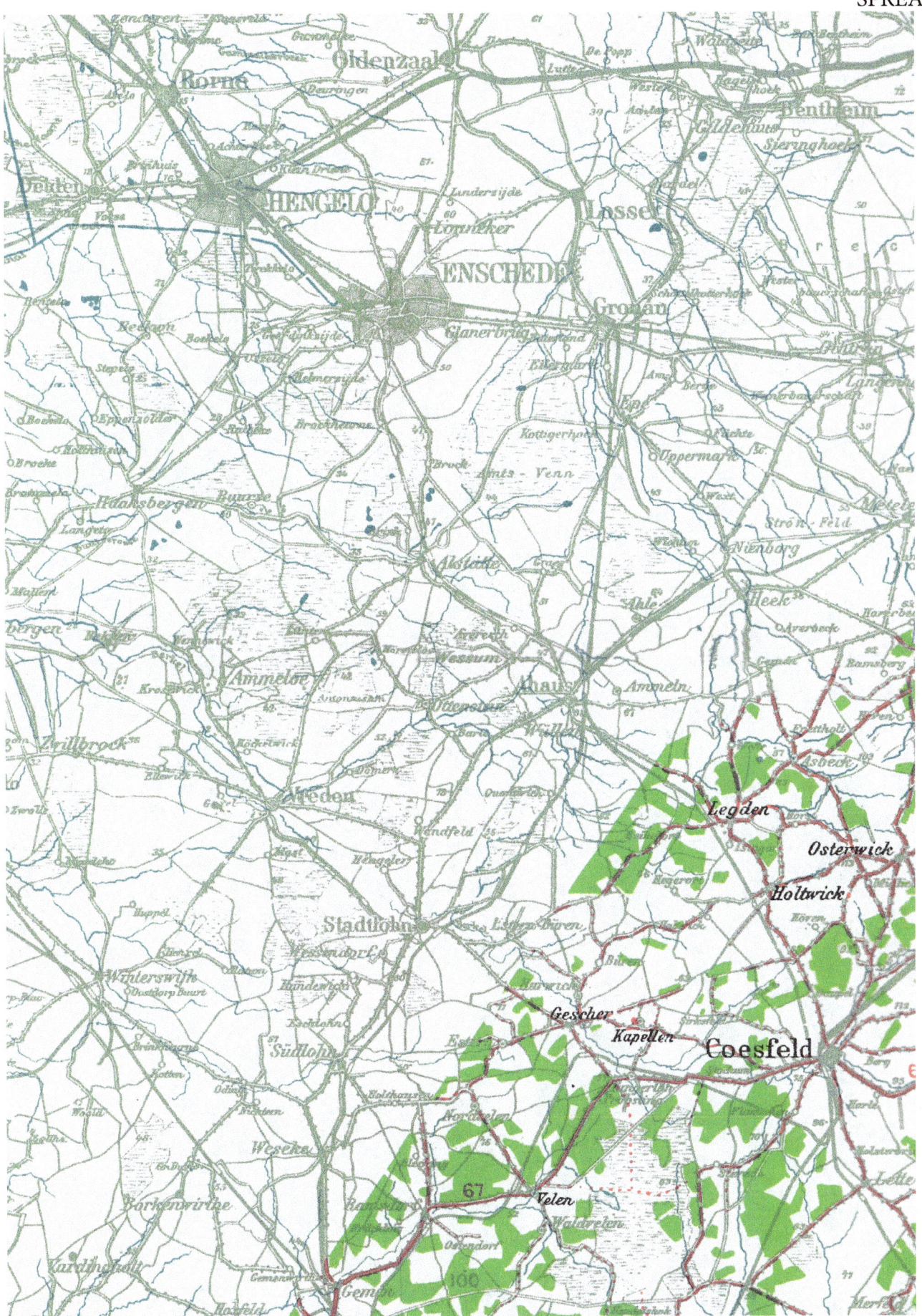

SPREAD 5

SPREAD 5

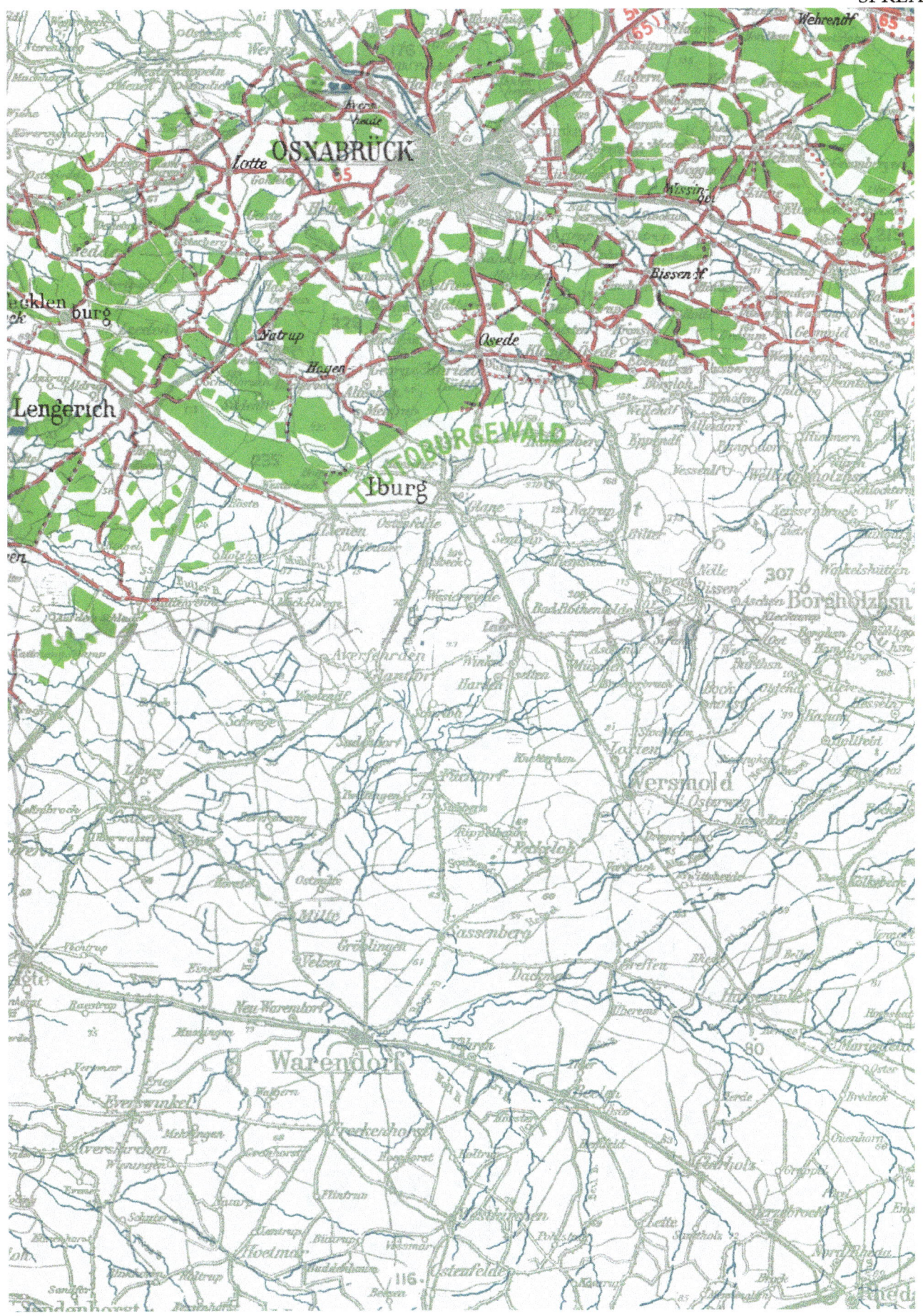

SPREAD 6

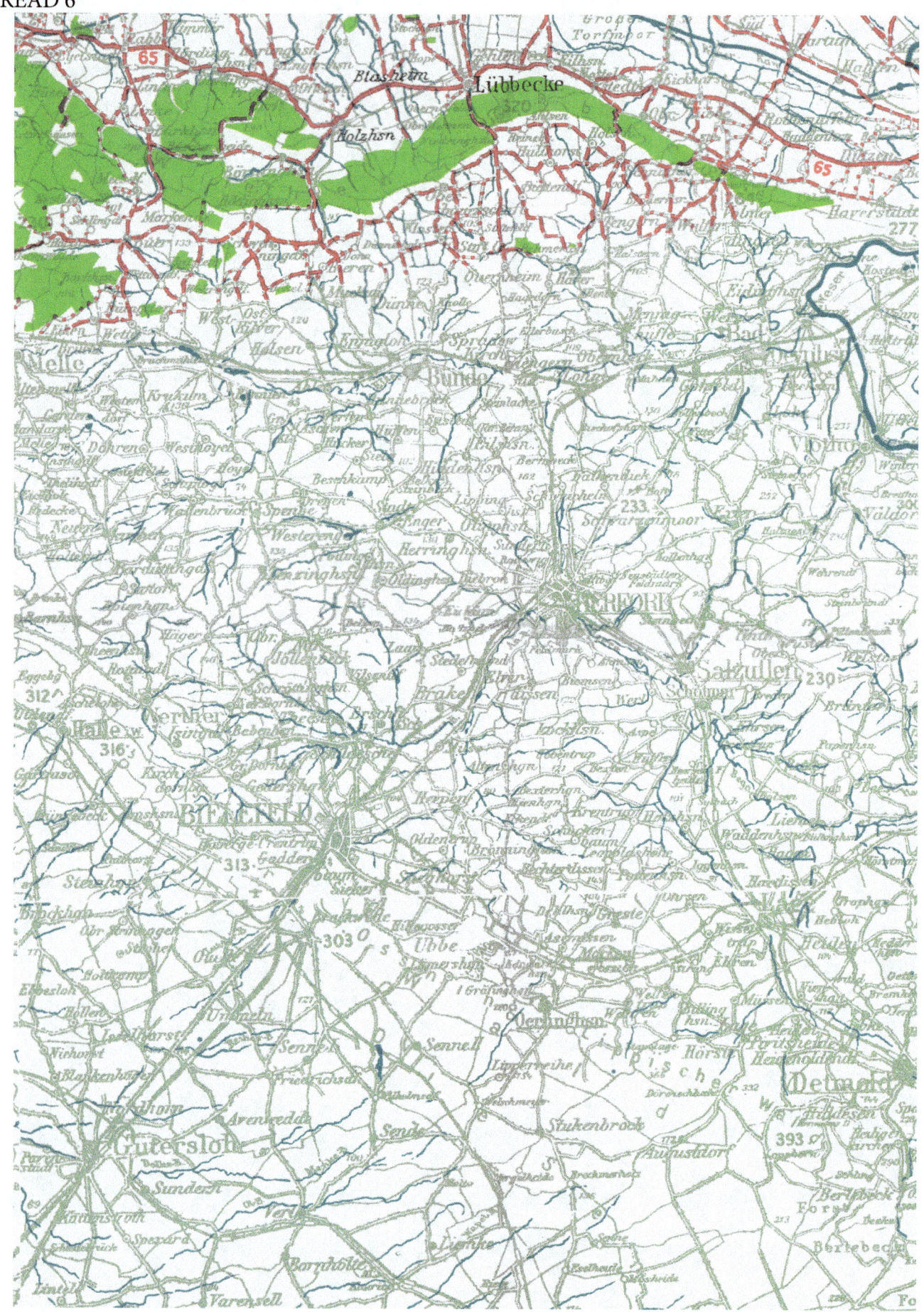

SPREAD 6

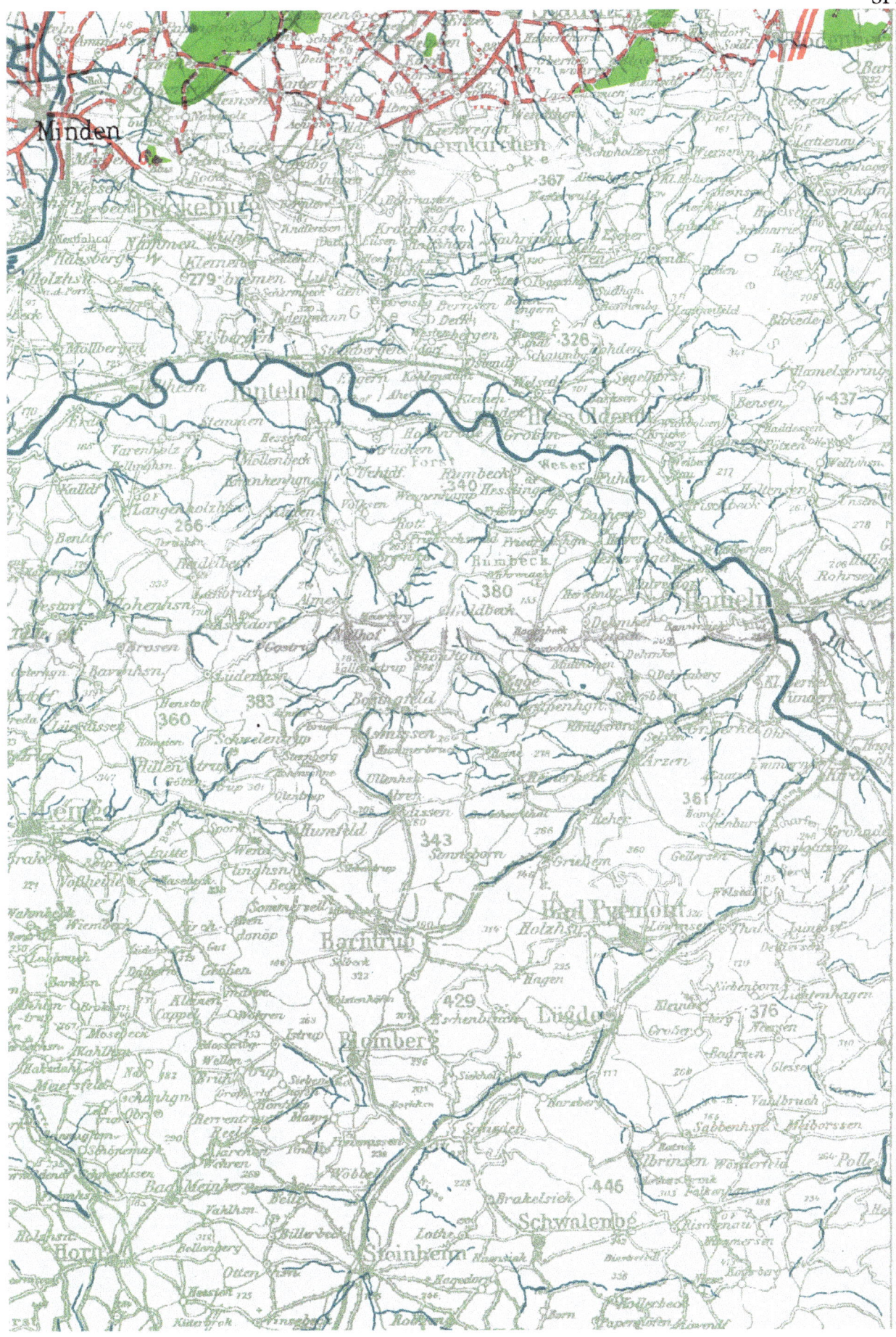

SPREAD 7

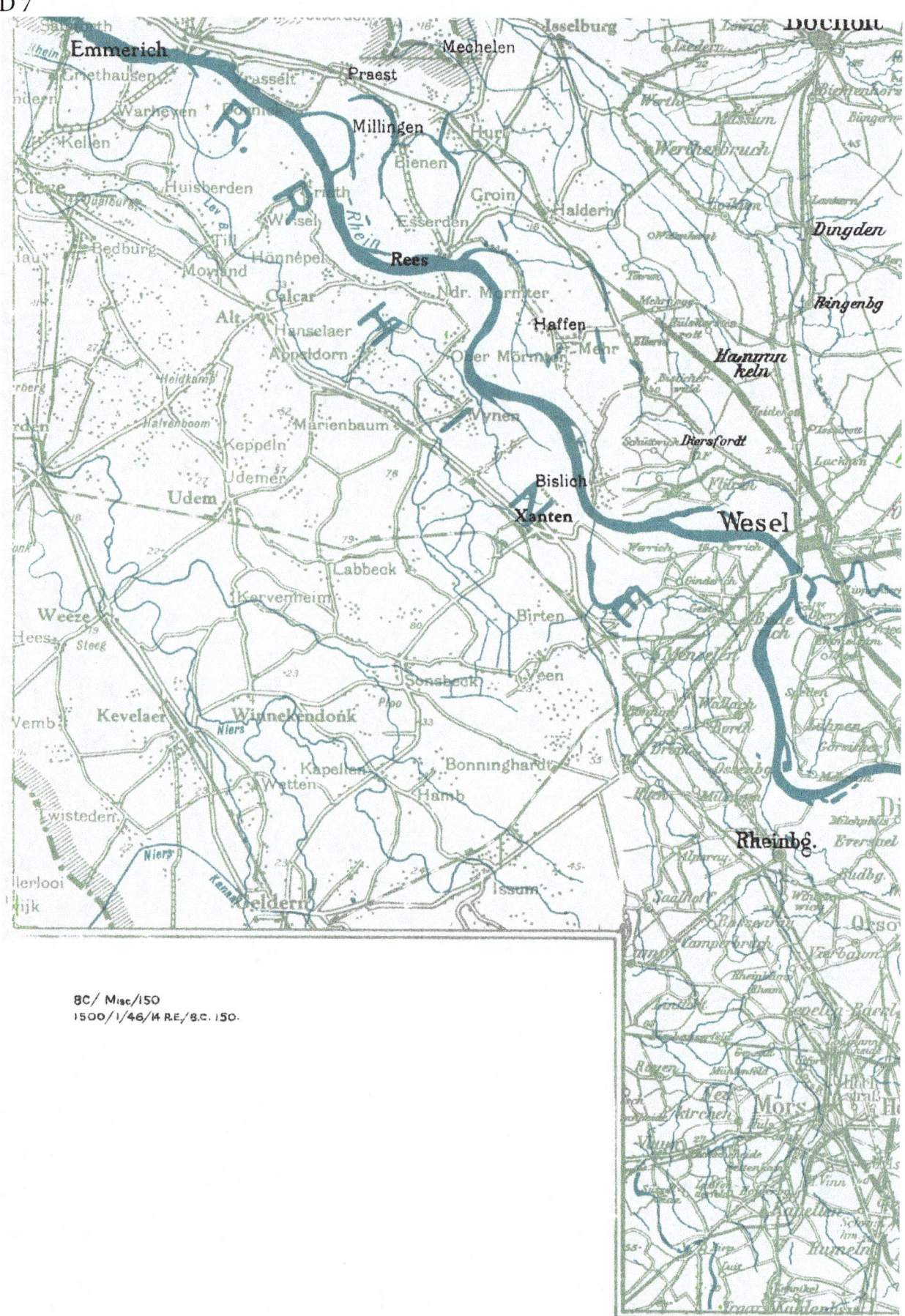

SPREAD 7

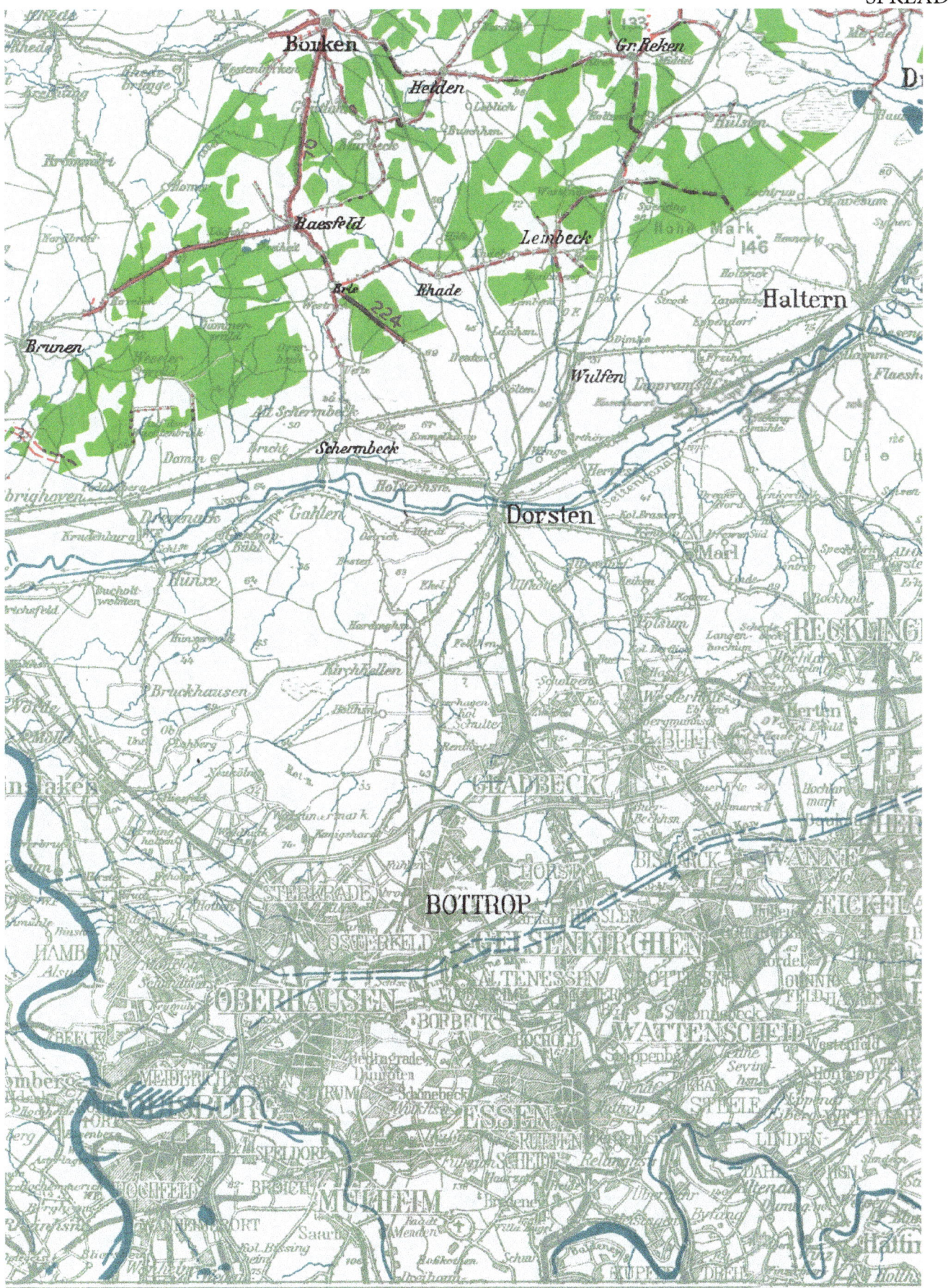

SPREAD 8

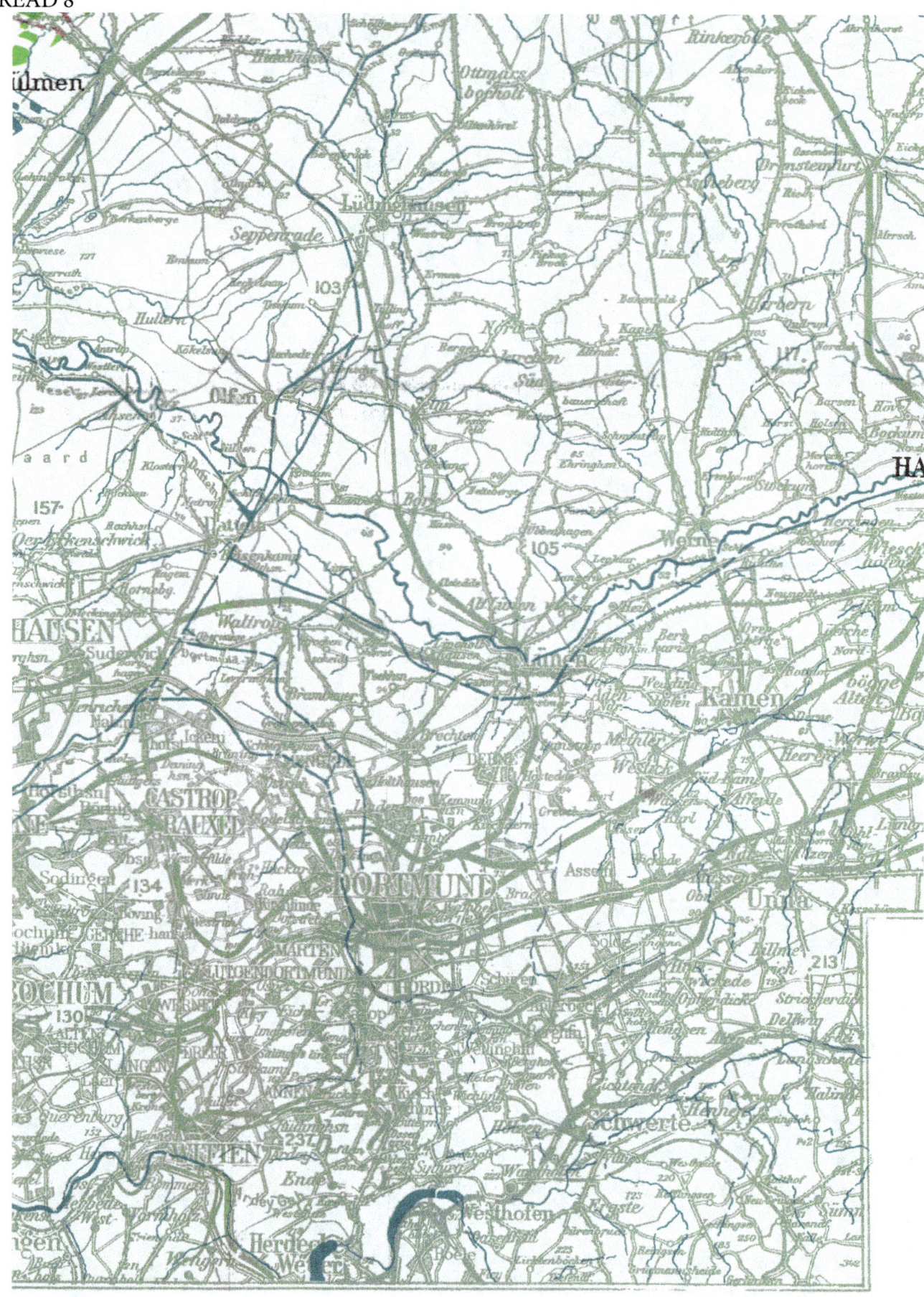

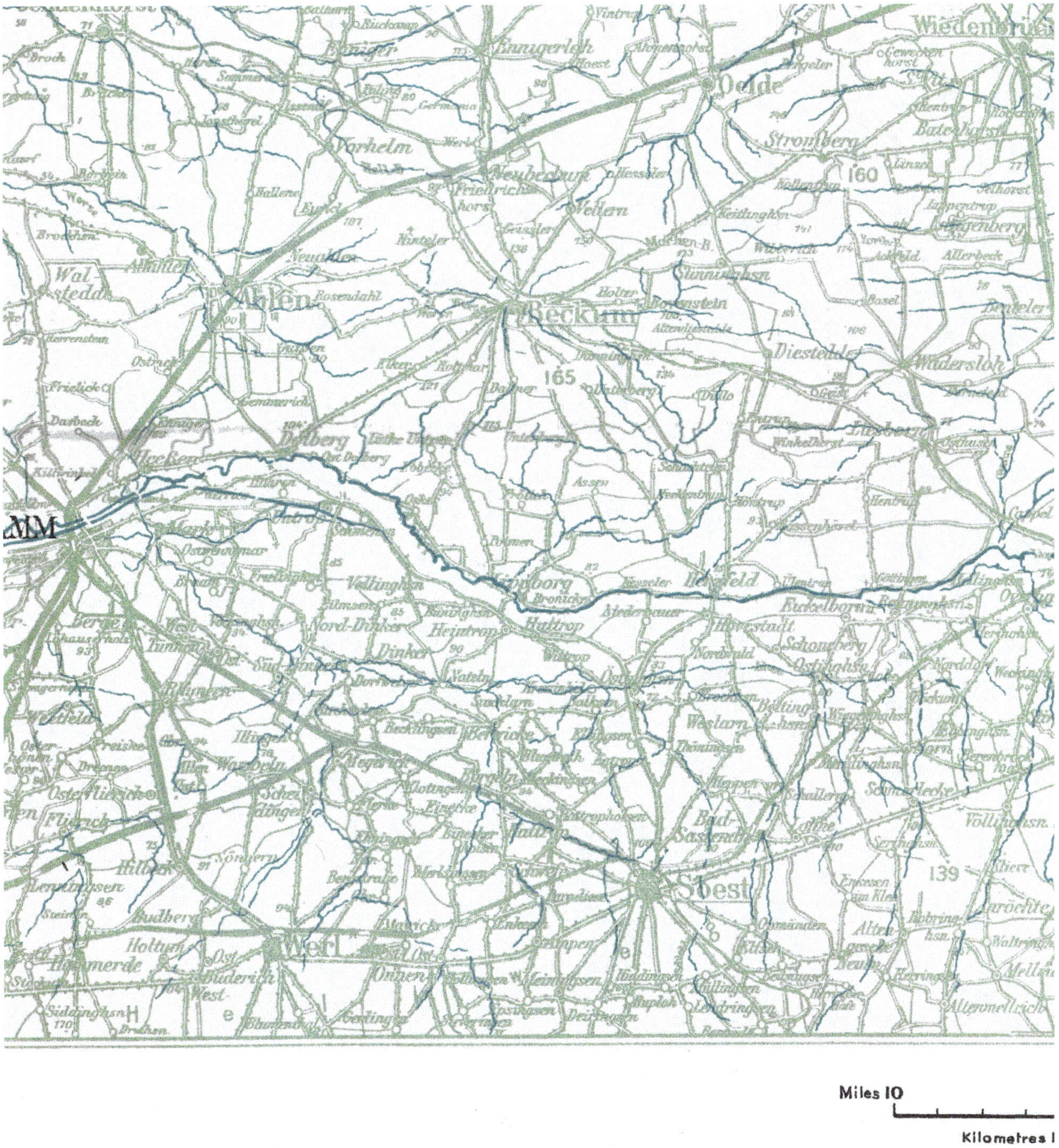
Ennigerloh
Oelde
Stromberg
Vorhelm
Neubeckum
Wellern
Ahlen
Rosendahl
Beckum
Sünninghsn
Diestedde
Wadersloh
Dolberg
165
160
Herzfeld
Lippborg
Hultrop
Heintrop
Dinker
Nord-Dinker
Vellinghsn
Hovestadt
Eickelborn
Schoneberg
Ostinghsn
Weslarn
Bad-Sassendorf
Soest
139
Werl
Büderich
Holtum
Budberg
Hilbeck
Flierich
Anröchte
Miles 10
Kilometres

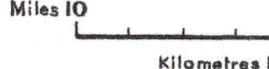

SPREAD 9

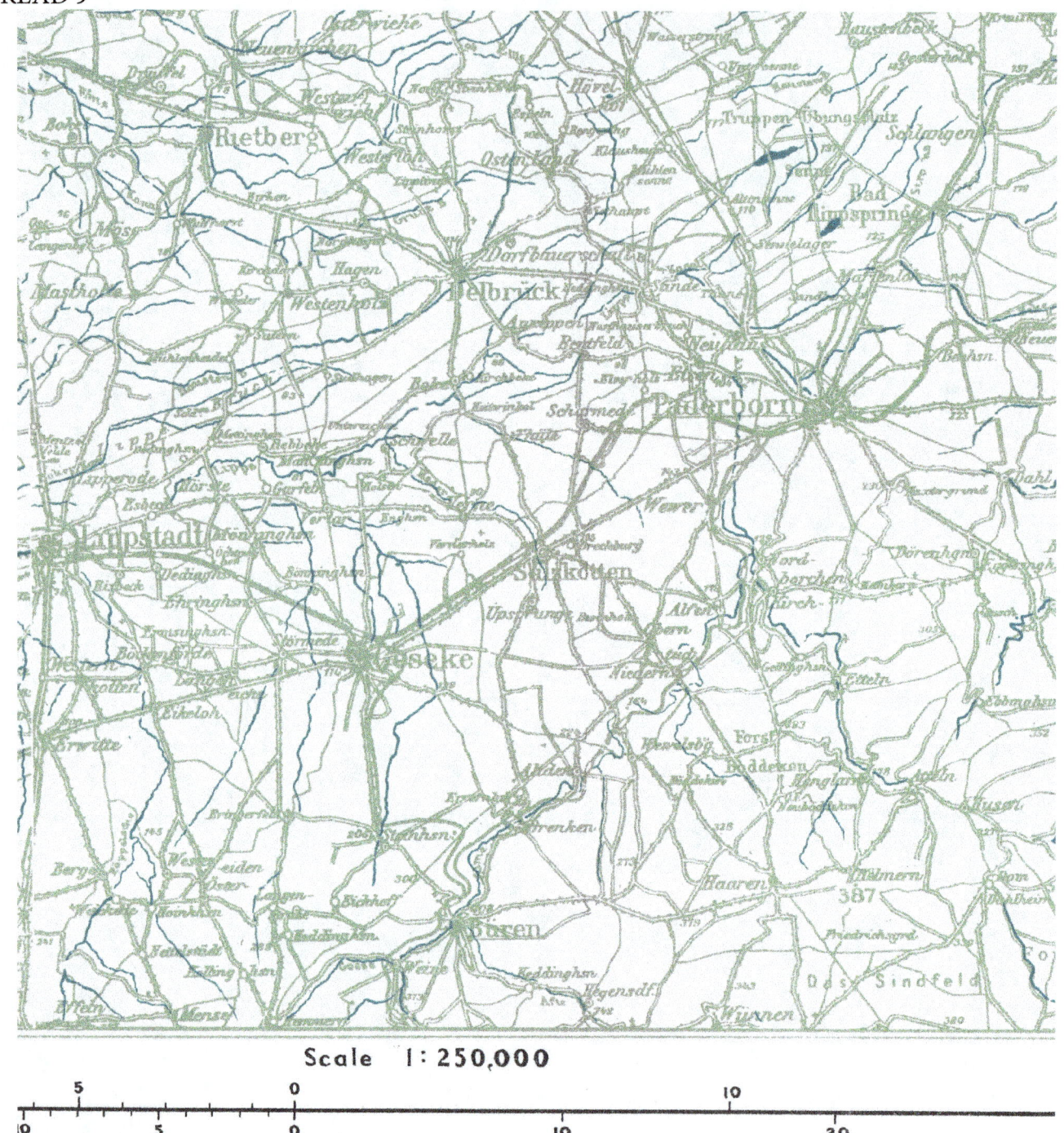

Scale 1:250,000

SPREAD 9

20 Miles
30 Kilometres

A FULL RUN REPRINT OF SIR CHARLES OMAN'S 7-VOLUME HISTORY OF THE PENINSULAR WAR

Always in Print and Always Available in both Softback and Hardback editions from
WWW.NAVAL-MILITARY-PRESS.COM

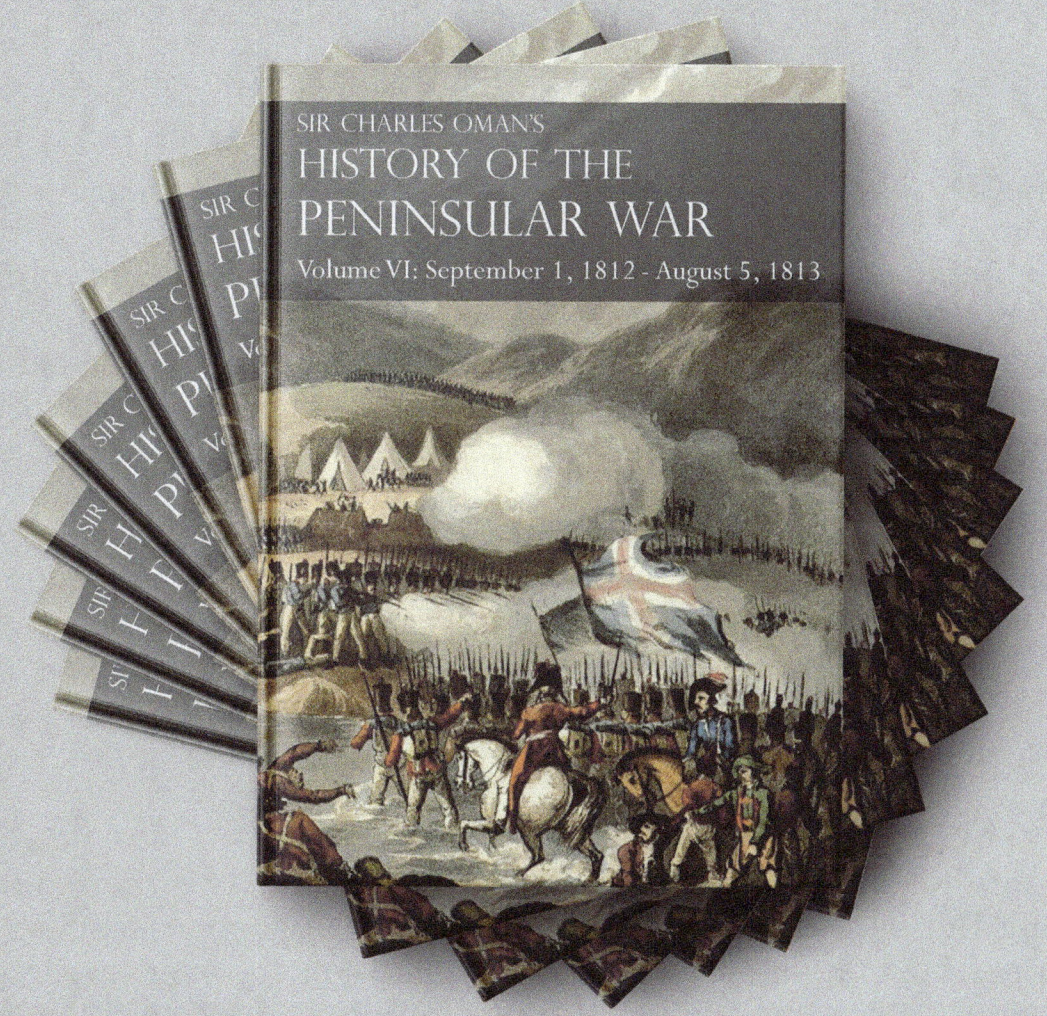

Sir Charles Oman's classic 7-volume History of the Peninsular War is one of the most important histories of the period ever written. The work of a brilliant historian and writer, it presents a large amount of detailed and valuable information in a very readable style.

Naval and Military Press have reprinted this valuable and timeless work in its entirety, faithful to the originals in all respects including 72 maps in colour

The 1807-1814 war in the Iberian Peninsula was one of the most significant and influential campaigns of the Napoleonic Wars. Arising from Napoleon's strategic necessity to impose his rule over Portugal and Spain, it evolved into a constant drain on his resources. Sir Charles Oman's 7-volume history of the campaign is an unrivalled and essential work. His extensive use and analysis of French, Spanish, Portuguese and British participants' accounts and archival material, together with his own inspection of the battlefields, provides a comprehensive and balanced account of this most important episode in Napoleonic military history.

The contents of the individual volumes are as follows

VOLUME ONE

of Sir Charles Oman's classic history provides the background to the war and its origins, and covers the early stages of the conflict. Introducing the subject and many of its main players, this volume recounts the French invasion of Portugal and the forcible deposition of the Spanish royal family, the beginning of Spanish popular resistance, the arrival of the British in the Iberian Peninsula, the first victories of Sir Arthur Wellesley (the future Duke of Wellington), Napoleon's personal participation in the Spanish campaign, the French surrender at Baylen, and Sir John Moore's terrible retreat, ending with his death in the hour of victory at the Battle of Corunna.
2017 N & M Press reprint (of original 1902 edition). SB. xv + 656 pp with 9 maps in colour + Illustrations

VOLUME TWO

The fate of the Iberian Peninsula was very much in the balance during the period January-September 1809, when it seemed all too possible that Napoleon would achieve control over Spain and Portugal. This volume covers the continuing Spanish resistance to French occupation, the renewed French invasion of Portugal, and the return to the Peninsula and subsequent victories of Sir Arthur Wellesley, including his outmanoeuvring of the French from Oporto and culminating in the hard-fought victory at Talavera.
2017 N & M Press reprint (of original 1903 edition). SB. xi + 664 pp with 9 maps in colour + Illustrations

VOLUME THREE

Covers the period from September 1809 to December 1810, when the French were consolidating their hold on Spain, crushing resistance and attempting to drive the British out of Portugal. However, they could not wholly defeat their opponents. The forces of the Spanish Regency Council, with British and Portuguese aid, held out against the siege of Cadiz. Wellington's Allied army fought a model defensive battle at Bussaco, stalling the French drive into Portugal and enabling the British and Portuguese forces to retire to the shelter of the Torres Vedras fortifications. Here the Allies' defence led to a strategic victory, blunting the French offensive, and ultimately forcing the French to abandon their invasion of Portugal.

2017 N & M Press reprint (of original 1908 edition). SB. xii + 568 pp with 14 maps in colour + Illustrations

VOLUME FOUR

Covers the period during which Portugal was finally secured from the danger of French conquest. French successes in Spain continued, but the army under Masséna was forced finally to retreat from Portugal. The Allied offensive began to gather momentum, although their attempt to recapture Badajoz was unsuccessful. Beresford's campaign on the southern frontier of Portugal included one of the hardest-fought actions of the era, the Battle of Albuera, and Graham's victory at Barrosa aided the long-running defence of Cadiz against the French siege.

Wellington saw victory at Fuentes de Oñoro, and smaller scale successes for the British Army also occurred at El Bodon, Sabugal and Arroyo dos Molinos.

2017 N & M Press reprint (of original 1911 edition). SB. xiv + 664 pp with 16 maps in colour + Illustrations

VOLUME FIVE

Covers the period during which the outcome of the war was effectively decided by Wellington's great advance from Portugal into Spain. The operations that
took place at this time include the French campaigns of late 1811, with their conquest of Valencia and the siege of Tarifa; Wellington's offensive, involving the terrible sieges and storming of the border fortresses of Ciudad Rodrigo and Badajoz; and his

great victory at Salamanca, which did much to decide the fate of the French hold on Spain. Other notable actions include that at Garcia Hernandez, and there were also smaller operations such as those on the east coast of Spain. Orders of battle, lists of strengths and casualties, and an account of Wellington's intelligence officer and code-breaker Sir George Scovell, whose efforts contributed greatly to Wellington's plans of campaign, are given in the appendices.

2017 N & M Press reprint (of original 1914 edition). SB. xiv + 634 pp with 14 maps in colour + Illustrations

VOLUME SIX

Covers Between the Autumn of 1812 and the late Summer of 1813 campaigning in the Peninsula took on anew aspect. From being a defence of Portugal and those parts of Spain not under French control, it became an effort by the British, Spanish and Portuguese forces aimed at driving the French out completely. Operations at the end of 1812 include the unsuccessful British siege of Burgos and the subsequent retreat; renewed campaigning on the east coast of Spain, including Murray's actions around Tarragona; and the beginning of the final offensive against the French, including the battles of Roncesvalles, Maya and Sorauren.

2017 N & M Press reprint (of original 1922 edition). SB. xi + 785 pp with 11 maps in colour + Illustrations

VOLUME SEVEN

Between August 1813 and the end of hostilities in April 1814, Napoleon's forces were finally expelled from the Iberian Peninsula. Wellington's army invaded southern France, only halting its operations when news was received of Napoleon's abdication.

The events covered in this volume include the British siege and capture of St. Sebastian; the final campaigning in eastern Spain; Wellington's invasion of France; and the last actions of the war in the Battle of Toulouse and the French sortie from Bayonne. A chapter on the place of the Peninsular War in history concludes Oman's monumental work.

2017 N & M Press reprint (of original edition). SB. with maps in colour + Illustrations

OMAN'S ATLAS OF THE PENINSULAR WAR

A Complete Colour Assembly of all Maps & Plans from Sir Charles Oman's History of the Peninsular War

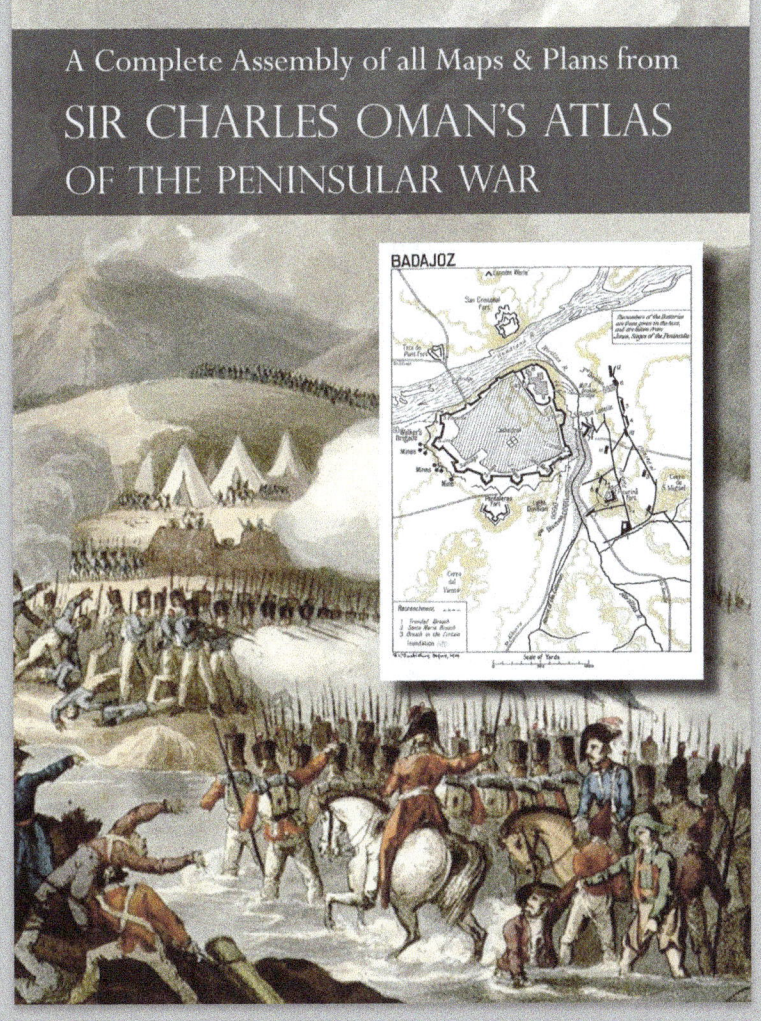

A full assembly of all 98 colour maps and plans (plus 7 in black and white) from Sir Charles Oman's History of the Peninsular War. The maps are in chronological order and include the famous such as "Ciudad Rodrigo" and "Badajoz", and the not so famous such as "Battle of Espinosa, November 11, 1808".

The maps are full size and faithful to the original cartography in all respects, allowing the reader to follow the War and its battles, campaigns and skirmishes, as the fighting and its various phases developed month by month, and year by year. This is a very impressive map collection that should be part of every serious Napoleonic scholar's collection.

www.ingramcontent.com/pod-product-compliance
Lightning Source LLC
Chambersburg PA
CBHW081842230426
43669CB00018B/2785